VIVEKANANDA

SPIRITUALITY FOR
LEADERSHIP & SUCCESS

Ultimate Spiritual Lessons,
based on the PowerTalks and MysticTalks of

PRANAY

Published 2025

FiNGERPRINT!
Prakash Books

Fingerprint Publishing
@FingerprintP
@fingerprintpublishingbooks
www.fingerprintpublishing.com

ISBN: 978 93 9039 109 7

Preface

Vivekananda bridged the ancient and the modern, the East and the West. He was a spiritual warrior, who in a short life encapsulated the essence of Hindu and Indian wisdom for raising human consciousness. His numerous conversations, talks, writings, and life incidents offer insights into some of the most important mystic secrets for human excellence. Especially for a globalized world, which he clearly envisioned and foresaw. This book distils the timeless values for leadership and success that he stood for, and presents them as insightful, easy-to-read principles that are relevant not just today, but for the future of mankind.

Vivekananda always led from the front. For example, during the terrible plague epidemic of 1898, which ravaged India, he proactively sought to help. He published the famous 'Plague Manifesto', outlining the steps needed to be carried out to meet the challenge. He himself was at the forefront of solving this difficult problem, and extended all help! Hence, we can see that he makes for a perfect leader on true success and leadership: always walking the talk through his own stellar example.

Pranay

Contents

CHAPTER-1

Don't Get Restricted by Ideologies

LESSON: The greatest human beings are universalistic in outlook. They have a vast vision towards life and leadership. They do not get restricted by narrow ideologies, as no ideology can completely address the vastness of man's being at the level of mind-body-soul! Swami Vivekananda is the ultimate example of an all-inclusive, vast-visioned thought leader and spiritual teacher. His message is to expand our horizons, beyond ideologies or creeds. He is also a true example of being a world icon and leadership icon, even though he held no conventional position of power! Leaders— and all those seeking true success—must embrace and emulate Vivekananda's vastness of outlook if at all they are to be constructive. This would allow them to be key in creating a better future for the world. Vivekananda is

unique because not only is he able to take us beyond all limitations and dogmas, but he himself lights the path through his personal example (as discussed in the preface, reference the plague epidemic of 1898). Hence, especially during tough times, challenges, difficulties, and crisis situations, Swami Ji's message is to be heeded.

One very important reason why great world visionaries, leaders, and luminaries such as Jamsetji Tata, John D. Rockefeller, Emma Calve, Sarah Bernhardt, and others were deeply attracted to Swami Vivekananda was because he used to constantly tell people that his method is not about a particular 'ideology' or a particular belief system. In fact, he used to say that Vedanta itself is something which encourages you to 'unstick' yourself from ideology, and leave all man-made ideologies behind in the quest for successful living and realization. It is the experience which is important, not the ideology. This kind of thing is exactly what drew great scientific minds such as Nikola Tesla also to Vivekananda.

It is this very *openness* of attitude that is key here. The most important lesson for true success and good leadership in our rapidly changing world is the principle of moving away from very rigid ideologies and moving towards an open, accepting, broad-visioned attitude. This creates dynamic leadership innovation, broader communication abilities and inspiration, as well as evokes the confidence of people across the spectrum.

Vivekananda might have had the appearance of a Hindu *sannyasi*, but his real achievement is transcending all sorts of ideologies and limitations which are imposed by religions or social conditioning. It is about whole-hearted acceptance of all existence, and not only about a method or a technique which we follow individually. Because no method, no technique, can ultimately bring you to a state of purity of consciousness. That is the essential thing. Not to have more and more ideologies burdening your mind and taking you away from truth. So the real factor for human freedom, mentally and emotionally, is to not get stuck on ideologies! That makes our spectrum of mind conditioned by the ideology; hence, it can prevent our expansion of being. And that is also the root reason behind so much religious and political conflict in the world: everybody is sticking to their own guns, and nobody is empathizing with the other. So really, existence is meant to be understood in a multidimensional way, and that is Vivekananda's main contribution. He always acted as a bond between East and West, between different schools of thought, and cannot only be looked at in the light of being a mere missionary from a particular religion.

What is really important to remember is that good intentions do not necessarily make us evolved people.

Sometimes 'good intentions' imply that we follow particular ideologies, but what this does is create a very institutionalized and dead sort of spiritual seeking. It limits us as human beings. And all limitations as human beings take away our initiative, our drive, our creativity. It makes us fill our heart only with ourselves.

So the future growth of man has to be in such a maturity of spiritual and intellectual ideas, that we are able to go past particular ideologies. Only then does something creative happen. Otherwise people get caught in old patterns. This is an age of innovation, and today Vivekananda's ideas are especially relevant. All his life he kept trying to influence people to move towards breaking their patterns of thoughts, breaking their patterns of conditioning. He did that to Jamsetji Tata while on the ship to Japan. And because of the detailed conversations with Vivekananda, Jamsetji Tata decided not only to put his mind to modern industry (which came up at Jamshedpur as TISCO), but also to set up the Indian Institute of Science in Bangalore, which in many ways became the Eastern world's most pioneering scientific research institute.

So too in the West. The whole tradition of American philanthropy which was started by John D. Rockefeller, was actually influenced by Vivekananda. It is said that John D. Rockefeller had a complete change of mind about what wealth creation means after meeting and deeply discussing these issues with Swami Ji. And following Rockefeller's example, great American entrepreneurs such as Warren Buffett and Bill Gates continued the tradition of giving back their wealth for the good of humanity. Because the whole understanding is that they are not to keep the wealth only for those who are within their limited circles. They are to break these parochial or mental barriers and utilize their wealth for greater human welfare.

So you can see Vivekananda's influence is far-reaching and wide. This is because great people have been able to see that he was a person who constantly moved beyond individual religious ideologies, and even conditioned ways of scientific thinking. Which is why somebody as deep as Nikola Tesla was profoundly influenced by his ideas. You can say, in fact, that Vivekananda was a sentinel for the coming atomic age which began with Albert Einstein's theory of relativity in the early 1900s. In fact, Vivekananda has written a lot about how ancient thought propounded all things as being infused with a deep atomic power. Of course, from the mystic point of view, beyond this material energy lies a spiritual consciousness (of the Absolute).

But besides all this, the whole thing is to go beyond our own self-centredness of ideology. And then only do we reach out to the world with compassion. So future leaders are those who can unite people in a broader sense than any particular ideology can. To take a modern-day example, you can observe a person like Elon Musk of Tesla and SpaceX. He does not seem to belong to any particular ideology. Therefore, people look up to him as a really positive global leader. In fact, in Silicon Valley it is said, 'Be like Elon!' Because only those people who are able to transcend limitations of thoughts and narrowness of ideologies become dynamos of positive action. They energize others. And essentially a good leader is one who can energize others deeply at various levels: intellectually, emotionally, and fire up their imagination as well.

So to go deeper into life, and to go deeper into your own potential, it becomes very important that you pour your energies into spaces which are beyond man-made thought-constructs. Do not let your mind be occupied by what others have said. Be silent within your own being, and then you will find that your own intelligence is much more than any accepted ideology. That is the way to find your own uniqueness. And that is what Vivekananda used to constantly tell people: to have the integrity to be true to themselves, because truth always seeks out those who have self-truth. It is the most crucial success and leadership trait from the mystical-spiritual perspective.

By conforming to ideologies, man remains engrossed in an inferiority complex because he is told to look up to something. But Vivekananda sounds the ancient note of the *Rishis* (sages of ancient India) when he says that each one of us can become stronger and stronger, simply by realizing that existence has made you pure and beyond all man-made concepts. In your natural state, you do not belong to any particular mentally conditioned concept or school of thought. That is all something imposed upon you. Be free! Be bold, says Vivekananda. And then the crooked hands of manipulators will not be able to change your individuality. Move towards your self-truth. Do not be cowards who take shade under somebody else's thoughts. Move in the direction that you determine, because when you do that, your journey itself becomes full of adventure. And success becomes inevitable. These principles are key to life and leadership clarity, decision-making for the good of all stakeholders and not just particular sections, and inspiring a positive futuristic vision.

CHAPTER - 2

Three Power Principles

LESSON: Swami Vivekananda's message is ultimately about unleashing that unlimited power within us that lies hidden and dormant. He emphasized the infiniteness of mankind, and sought to awaken that within individuals and society. At a personal level, a leader attains true fulfilment and success by being determined to unlock the timeless and boundless potential within. All things follow from that determination.

There are three essential power principles for leaders that Swami Vivekananda can teach us. The first is courage. The second is faith. And the third is strength. Now, let's look at the first one. Courage is the key to real success and great leadership. Swami Vivekananda says: 'The whole secret of existence is to have no fear! Never fear what will become of you.' So we can see that Vivekananda was establishing a warrior code of sorts within the hearts and minds of people. And this is a very essential leadership lesson: to understand what it means to function as a warrior. Fearlessly. This whole idea of keeping courage at the centre of all our pursuits in life is key to Swami Ji's teachings. And in this way, Vivekananda is very different from most teachers of religion and spirituality.

The kind of fearlessness he was talking about was a mystical or spiritual fearlessness. And such fearlessness is intensely creative. It is intensely capable of making a person charismatic. So for a leader to demonstrate fearlessness, to demonstrate courage is the key. It automatically and spontaneously elevates one to a great position of respect. It is like the fearlessness of the warrior Arjun on the battlefield of Kurukshetra who, once he understands the profound message of Krishna in the Bhagavad Gita, becomes very dynamic. Once again, he becomes that great expert archer which he always was, but which he had forgotten about. He comes back to his self-nature! So, all great leaders also are able to remember their self-nature, their higher self through this very step of courage. It is the first step for true success and great leadership.

Vivekananda says that at our core, within our very self-nature, we have a great deal of courage. That is the way we originally are! But in the world, we become conditioned to fear things. The child is conditioned to fear things. Our education process, our socio-cultural environment, our upbringing—all these sometimes become tools to inculcate fear within the heart of the child. And this is the most damaging part of religion! Vivekananda's effort was to take back people to the essence of religion. He takes us back to what the Rishis talked about: the state of *Abhaya*, the state of *Nirbhaya*, the state which even people like Gautam Buddha used to emphasize as being the first virtue of the spiritual quest and in fact, for all of life.

In Jainism also, we can see that the Tirthankaras used to emphasize fearlessness, courage as the first step. The great Tirthankara Mahavira's very name means the courageous one! The whole path of the Jain Tirthankaras was of fearlessness and courage. Similarly, if you look at the Sikh gurus, you'll find this element of fearlessness, this element of courage running through their teachings, running through the examples of their lives. So we can see that at the very essence of religion itself is this concept of courage. You can look at it through the lens of any religion. Look at it through Japanese Zen Buddhism, look at it through the Bushido code of the samurai warriors. It is all about courage! So when you abandon fear, you become creative, you become capable of greater leadership. You become sensitive and poetic within your being also; but most importantly, you become free within yourself to fight even a battle in a meditative state, to go into a crisis in a calm and meditative state. It all begins with the state of fearlessness, no matter what you are doing!

So in Zen Buddhism, a person could be doing archery, a person could be painting, a person could be gardening, a person could be taking part in the tea ceremony; but the whole idea is to provoke courage at the centre of one's self. It is the heart of spirituality. It is the heart of the mystic search. Disconnect with your fear. Vivekananda says that we first need to destroy fear. If you destroy fear, then you'll find that you are filled up with fulfilment, you're filled up with possibility. Then your body, mind, and spirit will act in tandem, in an integrated manner. So fearlessness or courage is the bridge which allows you to think and act in an integrated manner. Through courage, you are able to act as you think, and you are able to think as you act. And this is very important as far as leadership consciousness goes.

A lot of the times, we are thinking one thing and doing another; but that's because of fear! We are not able to live integrated lives. We are able to live integrated lives only when we feel the freedom of courage within our being. Freedom and fearlessness always go together.

If we are acting in a free state of being, we are acting in the state of fearlessness. And from a state of fearlessness, we move towards freedom, towards *mukti*, towards the ultimate freedom, towards *jeevan* mukti: freedom in this life itself. So this feeling of totality of acting with fearlessness is at the heart of leadership. It is the very essence of Vivekananda's teaching. It means being gutsy, having guts. And the connotation in yoga philosophy, in Raja Yoga philosophy is that down to your very guts, down to your very essence, you feel fearlessness.

In yoga, it's described as feeling fearless from the navel area. That is the key area of our being. When you feel fear, in English, it is said that you feel 'butterflies in your stomach'. So, in all the mystical traditions also, it says that fear is knotted up just below your navel centre. If you can free yourself of fear, those roots of your being, the chakras, the root chakra of your being gets strengthened. The same concept applies in Zen Buddhism of Japan. It all begins with this essence of ourselves down to the subtle energy centres of our being which we may call the root chakras. It is about feeling the strengthening of courage deep within our beings, feeling strong, feeling emptied of fear, feeling in such a situation that nothing can block our energy.

Fear blocks our energy! It blocks our energy at the level of mind, body, and soul. First of all, it blocks the energies of the chakras. The whole concept of yoga that Vivekananda used to talk about was the ascension of higher energy into the centres of the chakras from below to above. But because of having fear, your energy centres do not become activated. Now, Vivekananda had a revolutionary approach to religion. He said: forget about all the ritualistic nonsense of religion. That is a small part of it. First of all, cultivate the space of creative courage within yourself. That brings you to the state of meditation. Real meditation does not happen without courage. Move with a great assurance in your life. And Vivekananda in his own life personified the state of fearlessness. He always walked his talk.

He faced so many difficulties throughout his journeys: difficulties at the bodily level, the physical level, at the mental level; he was harassed also at many times. He had almost no respite, no rest. He used to say, 'I just believed that I am the child of this universe and I am the child of my guru, Sri Ramakrishna, and through that I found myself moving into a great state of courage.' So, it's all about the courageous heart. If you have a courageous heart, you are able to do all that is needed for your own potential realization and also become an example for others. And at the end of the day, a leader has to be a good example for others. The whole secret of dynamic action as a leader is this state of fearlessness, this sense of overflowing with courage that creates well-being within you and within the people you lead. Otherwise, nothing can liberate you. Nothing can give you joy.

Fear is the essential stumbling block between you and your ultimate happiness, between your normal state and the *Samadhi* state. There are only a few steps but the first step you have to take is walk with courage, walk with fearlessness. The whole journey of a thousand miles becomes easy if the first step is taken in courage. Let go of all that has been holding you back. Vivekananda says, 'Fear is unreal.' So he's saying that fear is created in us by human society. It is not part of our essential nature. Don't let it transform you and bring you down from your highest super-consciousness. Don't come down to a conditioned consciousness of how others look at you, how society looks at you and so on. Your self-nature is ultimately extremely powerful! Therefore, feel powerful at every level; feel powerful at the level of mind, body, spirit, soul, and so on.

Essentially, Vivekananda is echoing the essence of Krishna's message to Arjun. Krishna tells Arjun that the soul is indestructible. There is nothing to fear; even if the body dies nothing dies. The sword cannot cut the soul. Water cannot wet the soul. Hence, feel a part of this immutable, changeless, timeless, beautiful, vast existence. That itself transforms your fear into a singularity of courage. That itself is enough to make you evaporate all those anxieties and fears that you feel around you. And essentially, that is what a leader really needs. What is the action of a great leader? The example that a great leader has to set, especially during times of crisis situations for his team and for his people, is almost like sunlight entering a damp room. He has to bring such a vision! So when sunlight enters a damp room, it automatically has a drying effect on the room. It automatically brings the light of consciousness into the being.

So a leader has to shine bright with courage. That itself is the light of his being. Talking about things is one aspect; but that is not enough. Leading by courage is the greatest example that a leader can set, because that helps others also overcome fears. And when a team becomes fearless, then it's capable of manifesting greater results, greater hidden powers which it has within itself. People have unlimited potential. It is up to the leader, through his example of courage, to bring that potential of unlimited courage into action and dynamize the team, dynamize the group of people that he or she leads. Then he is able to move not only towards his own success as a leader, but is able to take the whole team towards a greater success.

The second power principle is that the essence of faith is very important. Swami Ji says, 'If faith in ourselves had been more extensively taught and practised, I am sure a very large portion of the evils and miseries that we have would have vanished.' The kind of faith that Vivekananda is talking about is faith in oneself. It's not about faith in God, an outside God. No! He says: first, have a belief in that which is real. Your own self is real. You have not seen God; believe in the real and palpable form of yourself. That is enough to start with! Have faith in your own being. This is the very essence of Vedanta. It says that only through self-faith can you have faith in the vaster, in the larger, in God.

The first step is self-faith because we have no real proof of an outside God, but we have proof of ourselves. There's no need to believe in a higher entity to begin with. No! That way, Hinduism is very different from Abrahamic religions. For example, it does not believe in taking a passive stance and believing what is said to you; it does not rely upon faith in 'leaders' of religion. No! It says that your own conscious mind should be suffused with spontaneous faith. Then it moves towards strength, then it moves towards a luminosity of being. And this idea of faith is essential to leadership. What is a leader without faith? Leadership is all about hope. And if a person has true faith only then can one have a sense of optimism and hope in oneself and set that example for others. Inspiring hope is a very essential part of leadership and only a person of great faith has the wisdom to inspire and kindle hope in the hearts and minds of the people he or she leads.

Strengthen your faith, come into a dialogue with your own internal energy, and then you'll find that fulfilment is spontaneous. There is no need to have faith in a greater power. Believe in yourself! Through believing in yourself comes wisdom, through trusting yourself comes self-understanding. And through self-understanding comes about a greater manifestation of your higher powers. Within your own heartbeat, find a synchronicity of thought and action. Great leaders have great faith at a physical level, at a biophysical level, at a spiritual level, at a mental level. Only through that is their higher capacity kindled. Only through that are they able to make people transcend ordinary and mediocre functioning and take them towards a higher functioning of being.

Faith is magical. It can make people move mountains. And the sense of faith and hope, optimism, and looking forward creates real respect in the hearts and minds of people. It makes them trust you. It makes them feel that their capacity for higher fulfilment is possible. It makes them move towards greater spiritual and material heights. Most importantly, it allows people to go beyond anxieties and to transform the awareness within themselves from an anxiety-laden one to a higher-consciousness-laden one. That is the very pith and core of great leadership ability. It is a core value which leaders need to have!

So great leaders and truly successful people are able to have great determination through faith; they're able to come to a *sankalp*, a will. The real will is created by believing that no matter how uncertain life is, no matter how insecure life is, you are capable of having immense trust in your own being. This creates a deep silence, a deep bliss within your being; and it creates tranquillity, calmness within your being. That is the trait of the true warrior—the tranquillity or calmness of the person who's able to take on any challenges in life! That is the state which Arjun fights with after the Lord has illumined his mind in self-faith and faith of the higher, through the teaching of the Bhagavad Gita. Also, you can look at different texts of India—the Yoga Vasishtha Maharamayan, the Ashtavakra Gita—they all say that having this seed of faith within you is very essential. In the West, Jesus of Nazareth says how important faith is.

So Vivekananda could distil and condense all these teachings from Indian and world religions and present them to people in a form which got them into the mode of practical action. He used to say: self-strength, self-power, self-faith are what transform you. That is his whole teaching in a nutshell. Because eventually, only a person who has these qualities can create true joy for others; else, a person is of no value to help others. If you don't have self-faith, if you don't have self-power and self-strength, how can you be valuable to others? And the essence of good leadership is to be of value to others. Hence, a good leader trusts themselves, a good leader loves themselves and respects the divine aspects of their own being.

Never feel hopeless; a good leader realizes that human capacity is beyond circumstances. That is the Vedantic position. It is also the position of *Sankhya* philosophy. In fact, all the Indian spiritual philosophies or *Darshanas* talk about this essence of faith. It is the essence of mysticism and theology itself. Self-faith. *Soham*: remember that you are part of the ultimate truth, believe that you are. It is like the old story of Hanuman before venturing into Lanka. He forgets his own powers and all the others in the Vanar army are encouraging him about his own past, to remind him of the valorous episodes in his own childhood, and about how powerful he is, about all the wondrous things he's done. And then Hanuman starts having self-faith and he grows into his great gigantic *Veer* form. He finds himself suffused with energy. He is filled with self-faith, but he's also filled with faith for his Lord Ram. So, self-faith is the beginning of faith for the higher divine principle also.

Hence, it all begins with faith. Yes, it's good to have faith in the higher power; but it all begins in the world of your own mind, body, and soul. The pulse of your own heartbeat is real, listen to it, respect it. The throb of your own being is real. Allow it to flower into a great spiritual faith within you. Then you realize that your potential as a leader can be truly met. Believe in yourself and then only will others believe in you. Never be hopeless, then only will others have hope in you. Remember that you're full of the divine energy yourself.

And that brings us to the third power principle. Vivekananda says, 'Never think you are weak!' This is the core Vedantic teaching he is giving. He says, 'The Vedanta recognizes no sin, it only recognizes error. And the greatest error, says the Vedanta, is to say that you are weak and that you are a sinner, a miserable creature, and have no real power. That you cannot do this and that!'

This saying of Vedanta has a very special meaning. Vivekananda was very fond of the Vedantic text, the Yoga Vasishtha Maharamayan. In fact, it was only one of the two books he used to carry with him everywhere. This is a gigantic book. It is second only to the Mahabharat itself. It carries the very essence of Vedantic spirituality. It is about the conversation between Sri Ram as a young boy and Vasishtha, the great Rishi. And this is the essence of the Yoga Vasishtha Maharamayan— the Vedantic truth that never believe you are weak, that you are hopeless. Allow the throb of your heart to be suffused with the ultimate truth. Remember that you are part of the ultimate reality called Brahman. Never believe that you are a sinner, that you are weak; because, as you perceive, so shall you become. Everything begins with your consciousness.

In fact, Gautam Buddha also used to say that our consciousness shapes our world. If you perceive yourself to be weak, you will feel weak. If you perceive yourself to be small, you'll feel small. If you perceive yourself to be a sinner, you'll feel a sinner. And therefore it is very important for the leaders to perceive themselves as inwardly powerful, inwardly suffused with the truth of the higher; because that is what they'll be manifesting in the thought, word, and action. Consciousness always creates its own reality; this is a fundamental part of Vivekananda's teaching. And this makes him a truly revolutionary teacher when it comes to leadership and success lessons. Essentially he was teaching people in the Western world how to become leaders in their own right within the domain of self-realization. What is self-realization? Self-realization means being able to fulfil the potential of your material and spiritual destiny. And it all begins with consciousness!

So Swami Ji's greatest contribution was to teach people and to communicate to them that they are not weak. In a way he was fighting against the Abrahamic religions which looked at people as essentially being sinners, and claimed that we need to repent for our sins. But he used to consistently say that you carry the part of the infinite consciousness within you; the divine consciousness. Hence, how can you be a sinner? You are imbued with the energy of the highest deep within your consciousness. You may not know it, but it is the reality. It may be hidden to you. It may be invisible to you. But the subtlest part of ourselves is always hidden to us. The whole process of spiritual enlightenment is to find the hidden treasures of our inner strength.

The shaper of the material world is always in the realm of consciousness. Vivekananda used to say that it's the subtle which influences everything in our life. If deep in your heart, you believe that you are weak, you will manifest weakness in your life. And what good is a weak leader? A weak leader is no good. Life in all aspects is influenced by the subtle; look at physics, look at quantum physics. It is the subatomic particles which are the shapers of material reality as we know it. Even the mystical world is full of understanding finer perception. Make your perception finer by understanding the core strength within you; and then you become unstoppable as a leader in life. Vivekananda says, 'Spirituality is non-mechanical.'

So we must remember that we should not

mechanically believe what religions tell us—that we have sinned and so on. Leave all that aside. That is not how Karma works in Vivekananda's point of view. It all works as a result of your quality of consciousness. That is what the Upanishads say. Hence, invest your energy into believing in the strength of your own being. This is the greatest thing that a leader can do. Through that comes about leadership, strength, and powerful manifestation of one's finest qualities as a leader; through that comes about charisma. Essentially, that is what leadership is all about: charisma and wisdom. Charisma by itself is not enough; it can mislead people. And wisdom by itself is not enough because even a person of wisdom who does not have much charisma, will not be able to lead people in a correct way. People simply may not listen.

Hence, it is very important to manifest this feeling of strength in the world. Not in the way that an Adolf Hitler does, but in the way that an Abraham Lincoln does. That takes you towards a discovery of your own depth and also into a realization of your higher leadership potential. It gives you an inward sense of stillness, an inward sense of bliss, an inward state of internalized joy; but at the same time allows you to lead people towards greater light, greater fulfilment, successful living, and so on. The shapers of society are those people who have been able to transform themselves into feeling that they have great strength within. That is the way that the Rishis of India used to imbue strength within the rulers, the rajas. Their whole function was to make the leaders of the kingdom realize that both self-strength and wisdom need to go hand in hand. When there's a balance between these two aspects, then society becomes balanced and everybody is able to move towards a higher fulfilment.

Essentially, the work of a leader needs to inspire people towards fulfilling their own potential and fulfilling the higher potential of the group as a whole. And it all begins by finding the sense of inner fulfilment, of inner courage, of inner strength, the sense that we are to have hope and faith. All these aspects lead to greater bliss, to more successful realization in the material and spiritual spheres, and greater bonding as a social or team unit.

CHAPTER-3

The Mightier Warrior is in a Higher State of Consciousness

LESSON: If we were to define Vivekananda's essential 'religion' or 'spiritual path', the best way to describe it would be as 'the way of consciousness'. He was concerned, first and foremost, about transformation at the level of consciousness ('chitta'). If change happens there, we are able to deal with all life's challenging changes and crises! Everything begins with consciousness.

Swami Vivekananda echoed the teaching of the Bhagavad Gita that to be a really mighty achiever or warrior in life, you need to be in a higher state of consciousness. That is Krishna's message for Arjun. And in fact that was Vivekananda's endeavour in his own life. He lived a relatively short life, but his constant effort was to create a higher man: not in terms of merely material success but in terms of a higher consciousness. And from that consciousness, whatever is done through a person starts becoming valuable not only at a spiritual or mystical level, but in his very functioning as a citizen of the world, as a leader, a team worker, and so on.

As Krishna tells Arjun, the true person of knowing is one who's very way of walking, way of talking, way of functioning, changes. So too Vivekananda was trying to make people 'know' or be acquainted with their own higher self, which resides in the interior of their own existence. He used to always insist that deep within man is hidden such an infinite capacity, that can spontaneously transform all his actions into becoming beneficial for the world.

One of the challenges facing mankind today is that while we have rapidly advanced in the sphere of material technology, we are confronted with the question of artificial intelligence and its perils. Hence the question of higher consciousness has become even more important. Elon Musk has said that artificial intelligence perhaps poses one of the greatest dangers to the human being. But the difference between all artificial intelligence and mankind will always be 'natural' consciousness. The need to raise it higher is imperative in order to meet all future material and spiritual challenges. Man's consciousness is the only true differentiator. All of religion and all of mysticism can be termed as a search for this higher consciousness. That is our main business in life; all other work is meant to flow through that.

As a by-product of this seeking to raise the level of our consciousness, comes real joy and real bliss. And vice-versa. From joy and bliss comes higher consciousness. So Vivekananda constantly advised people to work happily, out of a state of joy, but also to keep their vision on a higher state of being. His master Ramakrishna used to give the example of an eagle or hawk high in the sky: we might go into a great position or achieve a great height, but if the vision is only on the prey on the ground, then it is no point! You have to keep looking higher.

It all begins with not suppressing the spiritual part of you, of giving more expression to it. And then the practical aspects of life start taking care of themselves. Let's take the question of education, for example. Education is moving toward a new paradigm, where it is not just about information gathering. But if at all man is to evolve to the next level, we need educators with a higher consciousness of what man should achieve and how he should achieve it. The *quality* of man's functioning is the spiritual question. So bring more and more quality into the functioning of your being. And then all experiences of life become lessons for working towards higher potential-realization.

In order to be truly flowing in the work we do, it is really imperative that we do not judge everything only by material standards. But that we aspire towards a situation where we can go deep inside ourselves, and find that hidden power within ourselves. From that power comes all greatness. Power from the outside itself does not mean much, without expressing your inner power. This has to be emphasized: the ability to have insight, the ability to find your original self, the ability to move toward an enlightened state of being. Where tremendous radiance of your personality starts manifesting in your material acts. Otherwise the human being can never find true peace and true serenity. All that he does becomes purposeless and meaningless.

The purpose-centred life is one where you can find the depths of yourself. From that perspective, no work you do is superior or inferior. All work that you do can have miraculous results. It's simply the quality of your being which matters. All intellectual impulses of man are primarily a product of his quality of consciousness. If that is strong, if that is moving towards a place which is immensely creative and compassionate, then you can say that your inner guide is functioning. Otherwise man is functioning in an almost blind state.

No amount of technology can substitute the power of human consciousness. That is your 'inner kingdom'.

Vivekananda was very fond of Jesus Christ's words, 'The kingdom of God is within you.' He also related deeply to the Rishis' and Buddha's message which says that the enlightened being or Buddha is hidden within you. Vivekananda kept emphasizing these ancient teachings, even while clothing it in the terminology of Vedanta.

The beauty is once you attain a higher state of consciousness, you do not lose it. It becomes your real treasure. It becomes the most sacred and holy thing in life. Then all that you touch becomes luminous! Do not be enamoured only by the glitter and glamour of the world. Rather try to make the glamour of your inner world so bright, that you don't even need religion or spirituality to guide you. You become your own guide! And when you do that, you can be said to have truly evolved.

Evolution is usually taken as a word which describes progression in the physical or material sphere. But true evolution is always in the inner, emphasized Vivekananda. Out of that evolution comes all that is meaningful. It is like the metaphor used in Hindu mythology of the '*dasha* avatar' (ten divine incarnations of the Supreme). Each subsequent avatar is meant to signify a higher state of evolution: spiritually, mystically, but also materially. Through such inner evolution does the river of your life enter the ocean of cosmic being. And so entering the ocean of cosmic being, you attain all that is worth attaining.

The beauty about ancient India was that even kings were encouraged to look deeply into their own lives. In fact, there have been examples such as Chandragupta Maurya, explained by Vivekananda, who even at the height of his name, fame, and power, eventually moved toward the Jain teaching and looked to his own self-evolution as the only meaningful thing. And there are so many stories in Indian mythology which confirm this: that for true transformation of the individual, and for the true expression of your personality, you have to attain a oneness within your own self. That is evolution. Out of this inward centring and integration, whatever results come through your work become constructive, and not destructive. And that is the essential difference between positive, successful leadership and destructive leadership.

CHAPTER - 4

Expand, Don't Shrink

LESSON: Expansion stands for evolution and growth. It implies dynamic progress in every sphere of life: mental, material, meditative, and mystical. Swami Vivekananda emphasizes expansion of heart and mind so that your true vastness of self-potential can flower. His is the way of making the value of expansion express itself from deep within your soul. The spirit of man finds true success and fulfilment through expansion and evolution of mind-body-soul. Make it the very foundation of your leadership approach. It allows you to think outside the box and that is key for leaders especially during critical situations.

The whole art of spirituality lies in expansion. So expand, do not shrink. Expand at the level of heart, mind, spirit. What keeps people from expansion is simply fear—being afraid to blossom to their uttermost. About his own life, Vivekananda used to say that he 'burned the candle on both ends'. He always believed in uttermost expression of latent abilities. He believed in an expansion which meant giving of the maximum of himself, and thereby becoming enriched. Not only within, but also through relationships, through affecting people's lives, through reaching out and touching others in a manner which left a deep impression upon their hearts and souls. This principle of self-expansion is key for great leadership and success.

What is the secret of expansion? Vivekananda used to say that the problem with human beings is that they cling to things and to people. This very clinging attitude and attachment is what creates unhappiness and causes us to shrink. So essentially, adopt the art of remaining a little detached, of not choosing or judging—and then you find yourself undergoing an automatic expansion of being. And through this expansion, you become deeply relaxed and strong within yourself. Then things don't seem to affect you or weaken you. But rather, you are nourished by all experiences.

So, it is not a question simply of being result-oriented. In fact, sometimes being too result-oriented shrinks us in our psycho-spiritual capacities. It is an expansion of consciousness and awareness that is the sum total of the mystic search. In expansion is abundance of every kind. In expansion is the ability to grow to the best of our human consciousness. It is the virtue of being able to flow into new areas. Vivekananda, throughout his life, continuously kept moving around the world. He did not believe in staying in one place. He could have done that and be hero-worshipped, become a very materialistic guru. Because people were automatically attracted to him. But he always realized that this is not the way to expand. Rather it creates a vicious circle, a 'cult of personality'. So his way was one of continual flow, of meeting new people, of challenging himself to new things. And through these challenges of new things and new people, he was able to bring about natural growth not only in his own spiritual life but in all that he endeavoured. And till now—and in the future—his subtle influence will keep expanding in an endless cycle.

The idea is to expand the circumference of your being. But how do you do that? You do it simply with an attitude of openness. Of being completely available to actualize your hidden potentialities. Most people have actually touched only a small percentage of their self-potential. And the basic problem is that perhaps we have not sought to expand our beings beyond our comfort zones. So sometimes, we have to be less concerned about results, and more concerned about simply expanding our circle of life. That way, we can move on to the new. That way, we can move beyond the limited conditioning of the mind.

Vivekananda underwent many hardships. He could have settled into an easier life, but his way was of continuing to create bliss for others: through his teachings, through his hidden powers of awakening others to a greater reality. And essentially that is what every good leader should be: a person who can catalyze others' potential through his or her own expansion, and through the expansion of their psycho-spiritual beings. To make them open up to new ideas; to be creative.

In fact, being creative is the art of expanding. Otherwise, we remain very superficial. We remain content with what we are and what we have. But to move into new dimensions simply means a greater exploration. Now man is going to Mars, and even looking at the next planet to expand his material legacy. But it all begins with an inner attitude: about forgetting one's past, about being able to move on!

Vivekananda, the Upanishads, and Gautam Buddha, all taught that dynamism simply means to carry on walking on the path. That is the way of the warrior, and in fact of the leader. Through this act of carrying on— moving on—does expansion happen. Leave past things behind! Do not cling or be so attached. Do not hold all your energy within yourself: allow it to flow. Then even the stars won't seem far away!

It is said in the old books of Vedanta that spiritual realization is almost like a new sunrise. Where the light of the spiritual 'sun' expands one's inner being, and makes it full of light. So should be our own credo. Open your hands, and the universe fills them with its abundance! If you keep your hands closed, if you shrink yourself, you simply do not grow. Allow a reception of the greater power to flow through you. Expansion is life, said Vivekananda. Let go of what you know. Then do you become powerful. Then does your being spread into new areas. Then do you dissolve into a greater reality. And then does your energy explode into creative action! That is the very crux of the mystic search. But it also makes sense at a very practical material level. Because through expansion, you encounter that which you might not ordinarily have encountered.

So allow your heart and spirit to expand, and your mind circumference will automatically follow. People carry very limited ideas within themselves, and that keeps them closeted. We are our own limit makers. Go beyond all limits, says Vivekananda, and change your attitude from one which is parochial and inward to one which is all-embracing to the world! The old Indian mystics used to say that the whole universe is one's family, and that is what Vivekananda sought to create throughout his life. He tried to make the whole world into one family. One wherein ideas can flow into each other, and we do not remain institutionalized and closeted in our own ideas. In that sense, he presaged the 'global' age. That was his real challenge, that was his real mission.

It is the old Indian corollary of going to the Himalayas, to the open spaces where one's heart and mind can expand to the maximum. But it can also be done while living within the ordinary world. It just needs an attitude: that the whole sky is available for one. The Bauls in Bengal say that the whole sky is one's shelter and home! We are simply to look at it that way, and not just live under the shade of a very small and limited world which we call 'home'. The whole universe is our real home! This is the secret; this very attitude expands one's consciousness! If you look at the whole universe as home, you expand. That is the mystic secret which Vivekananda demonstrated throughout his life, and hence succeeded in being who he was. It is also one of his most enduring lessons for life, leadership, success.

CHAPTER-5

People May Not Be Happy with Visionaries!

LESSON: Mavericks like Swami Vivekananda spread the light of wisdom where there is darkness, so naturally they will have some people against them! Truthful and direct visionaries are always a threat to the status quo and the old way of doing things. Yet the only heroic attitude for leaders is to call out the unessential and non-productive, even if it means risking one's reputation. Have the guts to do so. Steve Jobs exemplifies this bold visionary leadership style of Swami Ji's.

Vivekananda used to say that when a true visionary appears on the scene, a lot of people become unhappy! In other words, 'a prophet is never recognized in his own land.' This is because the visionary is so against the accepted wisdom of the day, that his words become a threat to those who have a vested interest in keeping things as they are. The visionary goes against the norm, against accepted thought, belief, or superstition. The visionary starts talking about things which have an intrinsic value. She or he faces opposition. But the whole test of the visionary is whether they give up or pursue their mission. Those who can continue with persistence to pursue their vision, become the real leaders and truly successful people.

As Thomas Alva Edison used to say, 'Success is 1% inspiration and 99% perspiration.' So the true visionary does not give up. He persists, even though the face of opposition is there against him. The same thing happened with Jesus Christ: he wanted to break the superstitions, he wanted to break the taboos. And Vivekananda in his own lifetime faced a lot of hurdles. So this is a very important lesson to remember as far as leadership and the subtle aspects of success go: if you really want to be a visionary and do something new, never shirk or get disillusioned because of opposition. In fact, that may be the biggest plus point because it proves that what you are saying is of value! Perhaps if you are not saying something of value, there would be nobody to oppose you. Because you are not a threat to anybody! So this is the case in all aspects of life, this is a basic principle. It happens very glaringly in the world of politics, also in the world of religion. And definitely in the world of business, technology, and so on.

A lot of people are laughed at when they talk about visionary things. It is like that famous quote by the founder of IBM, Thomas Watson Sr., about how just a handful of computers will be required in the world in the future! In the same way, Steve Jobs in his second coming at Apple was laughed at by some very pioneering technology visionaries themselves. But he persisted, and that's why he became a true world legend. In the realm of sports, Muhammad Ali is a great example of this sort of persistence. He came back to reclaim his crown.

So sometimes the second coming or success after failure is true and enduring success. This is a very basic principle. Do not be disillusioned by people who are not happy with you: that is the way of visionaries, they have to undergo such a test in order for their work to be truly enduring. Care about the important things, and not about these unessential things.

There is another thing you should remember in life: it is often friction or clash of opposites which creates a greater energy. It's like the principle of the Big Bang: two different phenomena clash, and out of that comes all creation or the universe. Or two flint stones which you rub together to produce fire. In the same way, the human spirit often gets energized through the principle of clash.

When it is up against a challenge, when it has challenged the notions of humanity, is when the psycho-spiritual evolution of a human being happens.

So be completely unburdened of self-doubt, even if you are facing opposition from others. It is very important to believe that even if you are one individual against the whole majority, you can still be on the side of joy, creativity, productivity, and so on. Try and understand that this attitude of not giving in to the different voices which oppose you is what truly keeps a person going. This happens to a degree where you become not only more productive, but perhaps also far more able to look at the long-term.

What is vision? Vision is the ability to see into the future, and the visionary contributes creatively to it in some manner. Vivekananda was very confident that his vision would be a catalyst to bring people together, and to spread the light of Eastern mysticism in the West. He was such a visionary that he also presaged the coming atomic age. And that too at a time when religion did not have any connotation of science in it. What he did was that he bridged the ancient and the most modern. That was his true vision. He bridged Vedanta with cosmic concepts of energy. He spoke of how matter, energy, and consciousness behave and combine to produce the phenomenon of reality. And while at that time a lot of his scientific ideas did not go so much into the popular domain as did his spiritual ideas, there were some visionaries like Tesla who were deeply influenced by this vision. And that led to a quantum leap in the possibilities of science and technology. You see, it followed a cycle. The moment Nikola Tesla was inspired by Vivekananda, he contemplated things which were otherwise not very likely during that period (the late nineteenth century). But his findings about energy, about electricity, actually began to transform the world! In fact, his concept of alternating current of electricity (AC) was in many ways influenced by Vivekananda's view of *prana,* electricity, and so on, at the cosmic level. And Tesla's model proved to be more successful than Edison's model of direct current (DC). Tesla himself in his life was condemned and laughed at many times, but he continued. The basic principle is the same: it all begins with the ability to withstand criticism, if at all you are to become a true visionary in life.

CHAPTER-6

Take Work as Play (Leela)

LESSON: Playfully creative leaders can be dangerously productive, as they are always challenging the current stakeholders! In Vivekananda's vision, the divine is always playfully creative, and so must we be as leaders.

Throughout his life, Swami Vivekananda insisted that the work he was doing was actually being done by the divine power 'channelled' through his late master Sri Ramakrishna. In other words, Vivekananda strongly believed in the concept of *leela* which Krishna describes and exhibits through his divine avatar. The concept of leela means that everything is a play of the divine, and that we are only channels through which this play is enacted in the world. So Vivekananda never felt a sense of 'doership' for his work. He always said it was the spiritual master who made him function, and that it was the leela of the master functioning through him. He took his own life and work as a simple channel for something greater than himself, and in so doing created a strongly positive psycho-spiritual vibration wherever he went.

What this teaches us is that our work and our existence is maximized when we consciously allow the divine to express itself through what we do. Through this attitude, one is able to look at 'work' as a rejoicing and a celebration of the cosmos itself! Real religion lies in renouncing our attachment to our work. In other words, work as if what is being done is not of your own doing or of your own thinking, but is rather simply an expression of divine love functioning through you. In that manner no work will seem a burden, no work will tire you. The work itself becomes worship and meditative in nature!

So this was the spirit which Swami Ji sought to inculcate through the entire mission he founded. To the monks (sannyasis) he used to say that even our most serious duties need to be performed in a way where the sense of 'doership' completely disappears. Otherwise there is a lingering ego, that *we* are doing the work. The 'we' is to be replaced with a feeling of working as if a greater will and power flows through us. That way you keep moving dynamically, but without egoic motivation. Do not let the sense of ego confine you and make you believe that you are limited by position, recognition, or circumstances.

All identifications of position and power are simply creations of the human being. Hence, they do not have an ultimate reality. The problem with sometimes taking duty too seriously is that we get bound down by ideology, we get bound down by ideas about who we are and our 'mission' to accomplish. But the whole idea should be to share your being in a manner which is completely free! Give your energy and love to the work, but do not give your ego as part of your duty. And that is the whole problem with the world today: people perform good deeds and duties, but there is a sense of 'doership'. And this is what in fact plagues the question of leadership most of all. Because leaders on a power trip start believing that it is they who are responsible for doing good. They often take the credit for themselves. And then what happens is that the ego creeps in.

The very sense of 'doership' is to be renounced. That is the most essential Vedic idea of Karma Yoga. So true Karma Yoga in the way Swami Ji looked at it, requires this: the intellectual idea that you are the 'doer' needs to be replaced with the existential idea that you are simply an expression of a greater reality. Through this understanding, you function in a much vaster way, as an intrinsic part of the cosmic order. And that is what it means to be a real yogi or a real sannyasi. Where your false identities are shed, and you do not define yourself by small truths. But rather you go into a situation where you act out of a totality of being, and not just out of your own thoughts. This very acting out of totality of being implies an energetic and effortless 'playful' quality. And all truly great acts are born out of this effortless and playful intuitive quality. Otherwise, you will not be able to work out of an inner creative integrity. You would work according to false faces and masks: to want to attain name, fame, and so on. But true success—from the mystical point of view which Swami Ji used to talk about—is really a product of sharing your best capacities easily and effortlessly. That is the state of play, that is the state of leela. And through this state you come to the understanding that you become really fulfilled only when you do not function out of a competitive ego. So competitive ego is anathema to the very idea of Karma Yoga. Do not let the ego rest heavily in yourself.

Unburden yourself of the ego, and you become released from the idea of 'work' and 'non-work', action and inaction. You then move towards a situation where your inner being relates to the vast truth of the universe, and you can feel this indestructible power of the universe arising and overflowing in you. And when the power thus flows, you rapidly move towards success in every sphere of your life.

CHAPTER-7

Infinity Is Your Inner Being

LESSON: The hidden power of the infinite element behind the cosmos is within you! Never doubt that. This is the most key lesson to learn from Swami Ji, especially when you are faced with tough leadership issues and problems, that require effective decision-making.

Vivekananda used to emphasize the old Vedantic teaching that infinity *(ananta)* and endless power *(asheshbal)* are what comprise your inner being. And to know that truth is really to know yourself. Without knowing that, you are just burdened with a misconception about yourself, of being limited. And then you cannot go to any higher state.

Knowing that infinity is your inner being is the way to find oneness with the cosmos. And through that finding of oneness with the cosmos arises a deep sense of power, and a deep sense of relaxation about yourself. For the first time, you feel the ecstasy of your inner being, your own individuality and uniqueness. For the first time, you find an ecstasy in life and a meaningful purpose in life. Vivekananda kept emphasizing this Vedantic truth, whether he was in the West or in the East. It is a constant refrain in his teaching.

The whole idea is that power cannot be given to you from your position or outward success. Power is something which arises within your consciousness, and then do you become filled with light. That is the secret of charisma which all good leaders have. They feel the self's power. And that is the secret which all truly successful people encounter in their lives.

So the process is from the interior to the exterior: what you manifest within your consciousness expresses itself in the success of your outer material work. Hence the main learning is that you do not prevent yourself from knowing your infinity of intelligence. That which is called 'mysticism' or 'spirituality' is really a question of realizing yourself as infinity, and allowing this realization to overflow in all the various dimensions of your life. Then do you live life to its real intensity and joy.

And this truth of your being cannot be conveyed to you by anybody else. It cannot be realized through what others say; it is only in listening to your own self, of going deep into yourself, that creates an objective realization of who you are. Hence the importance of the meditative attitude and the contemplative attitude in life.

Vivekananda used to say that the biggest revelations in life are revelations about your own selves. Then only do you have the power to take on responsibilities in the material world. Otherwise our work will remain very superficial and not attain real peak of success. To be a positive leader and successful in life is really a by-product of inner transformation, of turning the darkness within yourself into a light of self-understanding. Then does the flower of your spirit truly blossom and spread its fragrance through the work you do. All impactful work is done as a result of such clarity of consciousness. It is not a question about being clever or skilled in your work. The spiritual attitude is to find immeasurable infinity and sacred quality within yourself through the act of insight. And that is your most precious treasure, which manifests as the impactful work you do in the world.

So you are to know your own inner vitality. You are to know the depths of yourself, in order to act through these depths. Otherwise you never truly act out of depth; you act out of a very mundane and limited sphere of intelligence and energy. The way to tap deep into yourself is really to go back to the roots of your natural self. And your natural self, according to the Vedantic view, is one of infinity. Then you can do things without any tension; then do you do things in an effortless way. Because you are functioning out of a power which is vast in its naturalness. So the anxiety-ridden and tense action gets converted into a very beautiful flow of your natural being.

All real discovery happens within the interior aspect of the human being, within the realm of spirit or soul. Man is deep in his misunderstanding of who he really is. He is asleep to the infinity within himself. He is said to be in a dream, and the spiritual or mystical state is the ability to awaken from this 'dream' and find true awareness. It is like watching a play or a show. If you allow yourself to become identified with the play or the show that you are watching, you do not really function out of an inner awareness of who you are. Remember that your part in life is merely to be witnesses to this divine play or show which is going on in existence. The real thing is that you can see through this show, and realize that behind it rests the infinite universal consciousness of the cosmic entity. Universal consciousness is the whole aim of spirituality, and through understanding universal consciousness your limited ideas about success start changing. You realize that you are here to not function out of ego, but to be part of the greater happening of the universe. So doing, you become joyous and happy in your day-to-day acts.

And this joy, happiness, and sense of contentment are the very hallmark of the yogi and the *sannyasin*.

It doesn't mean that you have to be a yogi or a sannyasin. It is just the quality of consciousness which you bring into your life, which determines the success of work. Vivekananda constantly drove this message into people, whether he was speaking to people who were living materially oriented lives or to the order of sannyasins (his brother monks) who were leading a more spiritually oriented life. He always said that the real thing is to seek higher consciousness, higher awareness. Through that very seeking comes about the power to be of higher value in the world.

A natural path of more dynamic action opens up to you when you realize yourself as infinity. And then you can achieve far higher things than you may have ever thought possible in your own life.

C H A P T E R - 8

The Test Is Peace
(Inner and Outer)

LESSON: Cultivate great peace within your heart. Quieten your mind. Then all the highest qualities within you will find expression. Peacefulness within is the perfect soil upon which true success and value-creation can blossom. Without finding your peace within, there is nothing to be gained: even the highest leadership position will never satisfy you! Pursue tranquillity, restfulness, and non-disturbance within: it is the spiritual secret for true success and wisdom-led leadership.

Swami Vivekananda used to say that the real test of your work is whether it creates peace *(shantih),* both within you and in the world. That is the real measure, the real barometer, of your success in life.

By this standard you'll be able to clearly see that most world leaders' actions are not really leading to peace. Hence, their actions cannot be really called 'successful'. A real leader is somebody who not only strives to create success and peace in the world, but even before that, strives to create inner peace. If she or he is peaceful within their own selves, then only can they create peaceful actions for the world. And the opposite is also true: if an individual can create peace within the world, this in turn leads to inner peace within the individual. So these are complementary processes. But peace is the real barometer and measure of true and enduring success.

Without peace, success is very superficial. The success which does not lead to a twofold peace (inner and outer) cannot really be termed a fulfilling or purposeful success. The meaning of 'purpose' implies that it should take people towards a situation where they can transcend the ordinary and move into the extraordinary. And the most extraordinary thing that action can lead to is the creation of peace. It implies creativity, it implies joy, but it also implies a deeply spiritual quality of awakening our finest values within ourselves.

So if you want to be a true person of fulfilling success, always remember that the test is peace. Not only for your own self, but for humanity and for the earth as a whole. In fact, this is what the earth needs more and more: leaders who can lead to peace and not to conflict or friction. The problem is that most business schools or schools of government and leadership do not use this touchstone as the marker and template for success. Everybody is more concerned about 'winning' at any cost. Hence the primary value of peace itself evaporates. It is sacrificed at the altar of success, whereas it should be worshipped. It should be held as the most sacred value.

The surest way to create misery for the world and for oneself is to carry out actions which create the opposite of peace: constant clash and friction for others. That way, you are bound to become a failure not only intrinsically and internally within your being, but also from the net result of your actions within the material world. You may gain in power, prestige, position, and wealth. But the inner flame of self will not be fulfilled through such actions.

So it is the quality of action here which is emphasized for real victory in life. And that is the whole basis of Dharma upon which the Hindu principles of life are based. Vivekananda used to often talk about Dharma not in a metaphysical way, but in a purely practical way, about what it means in a day-to-day connotation. And the teaching always was that we are not to waste our time in doing things which take us away from states of peace and bliss. The really important thing in life is the attainment of peace, not as a passive state but as a virtue and quality which we create within ourselves and within the world. So even if a person is a social worker, his action of serving others should eventually come full circle and create peace within his own self. Otherwise he's only acting out of a state of misery, and the so-called 'duty' he does in the world does not really lead to an enduring and lasting sense of blissful peace.

The human being is so different from any machine. Even so, as we move towards artificial intelligence in our futuristic world, we must also understand that a lot of the tasks we do can be taken over by artificial intelligence. Yet it is not the task itself which is important, but the quality of human spirit we bring to the task which will always allow the actions of humans to transcend artificial intelligence. Because it is the quality of spiritual energy that you can imbue your action with, which has enduring meaning. Doing your 'duty' out of an inner tension—where you are pulled apart internally—is not the way to create fulfilling actions.

The natural way is to do things with such a light within your being that everything you touch becomes imbued with that light. It is like the halo which the saints of all religions are depicted with. This halo of peace surrounding them—this glow of peace—is the subtle quality which touches others and leads to a chain reaction of greater and greater peace. There have been spiritual people in the world who seemingly did not do much social service, yet through their very presence and touch, much good work has been done. And the one quality they could spread through their presence was the quality of peacefulness: creating it within people, and creating it in the entire environment. It echoed around them.

A person of true peace is very charismatic because he is nourished with something of greater value than the material. And so he becomes a natural leader of people. Leadership is a very subtle thing, and the concept of leadership is changing very much in our modern world. But Vivekananda used to always say that the more we progress as a human civilization, the more important do the ancient insights become to us. Because the ancient insights of the Rishis have been distilled from thousands of years of human existence, and they are always enduring and meaningful. They talk about a synthesis of spirituality and materialism. And to bring about this synthesis, the bridge is that of peace.

Spiritual peace and peace at a material level always go together. And they both form the two horses of the 'warrior's chariot', taking him towards greater prosperity internally and externally. The real potential of the human being is actualized through vibrations of peace.

CHAPTER - 9

At the Source, Be Perfectly Cool

LESSON: If we remain cool and calm at the inner root or source of ourselves, we function well outwardly, and will take good decisions when faced with difficult situations. Vivekananda stands for this absolute inner coolness of the true meditator. Emulate this quality within your leadership style.

Somebody once asked Vivekananda what the secret of not getting angry is, even when grievously provoked. Vivekananda suggested a very ancient teaching: at the very source of yourself, the innermost part of yourself, you should have a place of such coolness *(sheetalta)* that cannot be disturbed by any outer happening. This is the way not only of the monk, but also of a person who seeks to strive towards spirituality, no matter what his material pursuit or circumstance in life.

It is the way of the true warrior. If a warrior loses his cool on the battlefield and lets his impulses take over, he cannot lead his troops to a true victory. There must be a space within you which is perfectly cool, untouched. A space where exists no agony, where exists no sense of defeat or failure. And when you act from this source, you become absolutely invincible in a mystical sense. Because it means that you have mastered yourself at the very root and source of being; you are in a constant dance deep within your being. And from this comes an overflowing energy which can really work to create abundance of every kind.

When it comes to the question of leadership, this is really important. In our day-to-day world, life has become so fast that most of the time we are wearing masks—a lot of our expressions are not entirely authentic, they are a little false. When people are angry, they put up a facade of a smile. But this is not the kind of coolness which Vivekananda talks about. It is about a totality of authenticity, where you are true to yourself. It is, as Christ also said, about finding the authentic 'kingdom of God within you', the real paradise or heaven within the depths of your being. Swami Ji in fact drew a lot of inspiration from such mystical teachings. He used to carry a book called *The Imitation of Christ* (there were only a couple of books which he carried throughout his life—one was the Yoga Vasishtha Maharamayan, and the other was *The Imitation of Christ*).

As a monk and as a teacher, there were many times when Vivekananda was in situations where he could have become potentially angry, where people were provoking him and attacking him in all sorts of manner (especially in the West, there was a lot of missionary propaganda against him). Yet deep within himself he knew and echoed that which Adi Shankaracharya always taught: that the world in all its changing or fluctuating circumstances is an illusion, and the only thing which is not an illusion is that source truth which exists within you and which is as cool as the mountain Kailash Parbat, the abode of Lord Shiva. It's that coolness which manifests on the face of Mahavira, Buddha, and other mystics also. It is that sense of indefinable calm that transcends your physical being, yet permeates your whole being. And that is what soul or spirit is, essentially.

The soul or spirit as described by Krishna in the Bhagavad Gita is said to be beyond mind or body, beyond emotions or feelings, beyond everything. Yet it is seeped in you as your very source. It is an inner space, and in this inner space your whole energy is centred. It is like an invisible solar system: a sun around which the planets are revolving. Yet this is a Sun which cannot be physically perceived: only its light and its energy can be perceived. So if you perceive this light, this energy, and allow it to function through you, then do you move to a spiritual state of balance. Yet this light is a cool light—not like the sun's blaze, yet luminous.

So let this quality of coolness pervade you. And then you will find a shift arising spontaneously in the way you function. The primary thing is the quality of our human spirit. Our outward behaviour and outward characteristics are essentially a by-product of what we are at our source. So let that become the focus. And when that becomes the focus, its quality of coolness will permeate all that you do. And really, it can be seen throughout history that it is only those people who can remain cool in the most dire circumstances who are the real leaders of men. It can be seen on the battlefield. It can be seen in great generals. It can be seen in great artists and inventors. It can be seen amidst great sportspersons. And this is a constant note in Vivekananda's life, a constant thread. He encountered so many difficulties—there was so much resistance to his teaching in places where institutionalized religion was very strong. Then what made him move forward with youthful dynamism? What made him ready to face anything, and not escape from any situation? It was essentially this quality that he constantly displayed—a blissful and cool responsiveness to situations.

Swami Ji used to say that while in the outer sphere and material world he is extremely active, deep within himself he remains in an intense state of meditation and inactivity. And so should the dynamic person be, no matter what his or her pursuit! Then only is true success possible. If you can bring this quality of being deeply active on the outside but deeply meditative and cool within yourself at the same time, whatever you do will start manifesting the highest quality, values, and strengths. Because you become stronger at the roots. No wind can destroy you, because your roots go deep into the soil of yourself. All the religions of the world are united in establishing this truth about the human spirit. And of course the ancient Indian Vedanta especially so!

Being Non-Possessive Frees Your Endless Abilities

LESSON: Truly great people in all spheres of life—science, spirituality, art, business, politics—have a certain detachment. This creates great clarity and dynamism. It is key to Vivekananda's Vedantic credo.

Vivekananda was once asked what the most important quality to be a monk is. So he said that not only to be a monk, but to be a warrior or to be a success of any kind in the world, the primary thing is that one let's go of possessiveness. Because if one continues to be very possessive about things, it simply means that one is confining one's infinite abilities.

The basic Vedic teaching is that human beings have infinite abilities. That is the first spiritual understanding. To release these infinite abilities, they must not be confined by the borders of possessiveness. Possessiveness is like a fence which does not allow things to go outside itself. But real success means expressing your energy to the utmost, in a free and clear manner. So it is not a question of morality—being possessive or non-possessive—it is a question of whether you are wholehearted in your living of life, or half-hearted. And anything half-hearted cannot take you to massive success.

From the mystic point of view, the individual is looked at as possessing immense strength of consciousness. So much so that even one considered 'ordinary' can become a Rishi (spiritual seer), a Buddha. One individual can encompass the truth of the entire universe. Such is our potential! And Buddha used to echo this by saying that within each of us resides our own Buddha: it is just that he knows he is a Buddha, and we do not know that we are Buddhas. Vivekananda was not only inspired by the Vedanta of India, but very much so by Gautam Buddha, as well as by Jesus and other mystics of the world.

So the thing which is absolutely clear is to know that just as the cosmos is throbbing with the pulse of the divine, so too is man's infinite capacity. But our only restriction on it becomes a sense of possessiveness. Because then we are not really joining our individual energy with cosmic energy. Non-possessiveness means you become one with universal energy; the doors and windows of your being are open for an interaction with the greater energy. And that way you transcend your ordinary mind. And so doing, you become more and more capable of achieving extraordinary things. In fact, this is at the very basis of what it means to be a charismatic leader, a person of broad appeal to all sorts of people. That is only possible when the leader removes his barriers of prejudice, of possessiveness. That is truly meaningful, positive leadership. Not the leadership which ordinarily we see in politics, but leadership which helps us move toward a better society, a better humanity, and at our own individual levels.

Possessiveness simply means that we are fighting with our own thoughts. We are trying to confine our own mental space by putting a perimeter around ourselves. But the world is a place of interconnections. And if you want to truly connect with others, you have to drop this idea of possessiveness. Then only do you become broader in your scope.

You can see this very clearly when it comes to relationships of every kind. The primary problem with personal relationships—and turmoil in personal relationships—is the idea of possessiveness. It is the one poison which destroys most relationships. At work on the other hand, people are possessive about their position, their power. And that way they do not really move towards their fuller potential.

The important thing to remember is that eventually nothing is ours: everything belongs to the vast cosmic panorama. This is the mystical and spiritual view of life. This is the worldview which frees your mind, and allows you to melt and merge into the higher potentiality of self and universe. Then do you come to an inner harmony with universal intention, and when you come into a harmony with universal intention you align yourself to that which it seeks to bestow you with.

Vivekananda transformed the lives of other people, not just his own. In that way he was a true leader. But this transformation needed him to embrace humanity as a whole, to drop his own possessiveness, and to become a person who could raise his consciousness so high that he could freely express that which the universe was conveying through him. And so doing, he became this respected spiritual leader, he became a master. So really it's all about knowing that a small cause can lead to great consequences. And for most people, the one cause for their self-limitation is this idea of possessiveness. The moment they drop it, they become more life-affirmative, filled with a tremendous courage. Because now they have a higher purpose. They enhance their view of life to be a force of good in the world, or to be a humanitarian, or to be a positive contributor of any sort. That requires a new vision for man: one where people are willing to interconnect in a much freer manner, more spontaneously. Through the spontaneity of interconnection, the resistance between people starts falling. And when resistance starts falling between people, then is established true communication, empathy, and understanding. Through that is bound to come about greater success and fulfilment, because then one becomes not only more attractive to others but also moves towards an inner space which is more satisfying. Simply because one is freer and more available to the world, instead of being confined by any sense of narrowness or possessiveness.

CHAPTER-11

Synthesis of East and West

LESSON: Being way ahead of his time, Swami Vivekananda perfectly connected excellence in material pursuits and mystical pursuits as being two parts of the same coin! In that sense, he synthesized and joined Western and Eastern sensibilities together, for the first time in human history. A leader's worldly or material fulfilment and creation of value is ultimately nourished by the extent to which she or he is grounded and rooted in spiritual values.

The whole work of Swami Vivekananda was to create a synthesis of East and West. Not so much a literal synthesis, but one of ideas. He used to always say that the East should be inspired by the material and scientific progress of the West, and the West should be inspired by the mystical and spiritual ideas of the East. So it is at this realm of ideas where the material and scientific emphasis is offset by the spiritual and mystical aspects of life. One without the other is crippled. If we concentrate only on material life, we miss much of the quality and purpose that life in its totality can offer. And if, on the other hand, we disregard science and material progress, our ideas remain very impractical.

So the idea is to create a synthesis at the level of thought impulse. Then only can we create a true meeting of both the aspects of life: the material and the spiritual. And both are very powerful aspects. Yet very few people attain a balance between them. Much of what is called the spiritual and mystical is disregarded as mumbo jumbo, and with good reason. Because there are too many charlatans and purveyors of nonsense in the name of spirituality. And on the other hand, there is this overwhelming scepticism of things mystical when it comes to academics and intellectuals. They have their own good reasons, but perhaps they need a little more openness in seeking out the higher and more subtle truths of the mystical domain. So really Vivekananda's work was one which encompassed the whole being of man, taking away limitations and narrowness of all kinds in order to make us broad and wide in our scope of functioning. And that is what it really means to be a successful person. That is what it really means to create value in your life.

Just the idea of material achievements cannot take you towards deep peace or contentment, and just the idea of deep peace cannot take you towards higher achievement. So this synthesis is the beauty of Vivekananda's teaching, and he did it at a time when East and West were regarded as never meeting. In fact, in Kipling's famous poem he says, 'East is East and West is West and never the twain shall meet.' So it was an age where the meeting of both worlds—or the meeting of both these ideas—was not considered feasible. But Vivekananda came up with a multidimensional approach, which encompassed both aspects. And the miracle was that innovators and scientists such as Nikola Tesla became his great followers and disciples. In fact, some of Tesla's ideas about energy about the basic constituents of nature such as *prana, akasha*, and so on, were derived from Vivekananda's teachings. Vivekananda talked about atomic theory in the pre-atomic age. He was so advanced in his thinking. Renowned figures such as Sarah Bernhardt, Emma Calve, J. D. Salinger, and others were great fans of his.

So you can see that Vivekananda is a 'bridge', so to speak. And really his whole work is about bridging both aspects of our lives. So within our individual self the lesson is that we need to integrate both aspects, and bring more consciousness to both aspects of our being. So that both can flower: material abundance and spiritual abundance. And when both these aspects flower within us, then can we call our lives true successes.

The miracle of fulfilment happens when the dance of the mystical meets the truth of the material. The whole idea is to change the quality of our consciousness to a degree where we can feel more content, more aware, and more meditative in life. But without taking away the quest for material progress. The most transformative power on earth is the consciousness that we are imbued with. And Vivekananda always emphasized that we are to pay attention first to our own consciousness, and then look to the material world. True value or true worth in life happens when you can discover the wisdom of your own interior self. That has to be the quest of both spiritual and material living, because then you are able to tap into your greatest treasure within.

In a way Vivekananda was offering a much more holistic thinking than the psychoanalysis which happened through Freud much later on. Because Vivekananda said that it is not just about the mind and its imaginings that we should be concerned with, but more about that space which is beyond mind. In other words, that space which is the procreative consciousness itself, and which exists within us and of which the intellect is only a reflection. So it is a going back to the very deepest portions of existence. And when we go back to the deepest portions of our own existence, we realize most spontaneously that there is real *ananda*: real bliss and joy. When we act out of this joy, all that we do happens with a totality of passion, an intensity of rejoicing. And through this totality and intensity do we come to a situation where our highest powers function into creating something much more than the mundane, something extraordinary! And that is the secret of great leadership and great success in every calling of life.

Life is not to be looked at as either one or the other: entirely spiritual or entirely material. It is in fact a balance between the two. Leaving one aspect out at the expense of the other creates a situation where much of our potential energy is wasted. We must be mystically wondrous in our consciousness. But at the same time we must not waste our creativity in vague concepts only. It is good to use our creativity in the material work we do. Vivekananda kept saying this to his brother monks—his sannyasins. He kept saying he is looking only for ten people who can do his work in the material sphere, and through those ten people he can bring about much good even on the material sphere. He clearly demonstrated, through his humanitarian efforts, that work on the material plane is as important as spiritual upliftment. He used to get irritated with people in his group who insisted on more emphasis on the spiritual aspects, telling them what good is their spirituality if they cannot help their fellow men. Through his seeking to uplift the downtrodden, Swami Ji demonstrated dynamism of both spheres: spiritual plus material. So his action was not only thought-oriented or consciousness-oriented, but action-oriented. And this meeting of higher consciousness and dynamic action is really the seed ground of successful living.

CHAPTER-12

Do the Essential,
Drop the Unessential

LESSON: Pay attention to the fundamental qualities of wisdom, courage, compassion, delight, and devotion in whatever you do. Nurturing the essential makes the focus of your thought-consciousness crystal-clear and undisturbed. It prevents you from wasting energy on useless things or on anxiety. This is very important for leaders, particularly when facing big challenges. It is a simple yet key step to your leadership success, as well as to your self-fulfilment.

One very important thing that Vivekananda used to say was that the way of the yogi as well as the way of the warrior both are in concentrating on the essential and dropping the non-essential from life. That way, much energy is conserved for you to do that which is truly important. It is very interesting because his idea of celibacy—what is called *brahmacharya* in the Indian tradition—was really about conserving energy so that you could move towards a greater release of your potential. That does not mean he advised anybody to become celibate, but the whole idea is that taken to its ultimate degree, man's entire functioning depends on how much he is able to drop the non-essential from his life. Then only does he truly fulfil his potential. Otherwise it is an endless loop: man is never satisfied. He keeps moving on with his trivial pursuits and desires, trying to obtain a higher position, a little more money, and so on.

At its very root, the whole search has to be one where you can bring your efforts and your energies into such a concentrated power that nothing can withstand its force, that you can go past all resistance. And that is the way of the warrior which Krishna describes to Arjun in the Bhagavad Gita. Vivekananda was very influenced by this. So he says that the mind keeps bringing up non-essential doubts about itself, and through this cycle of doubt, you lose your inner confidence. His mission in life was creating such inner confidence within people's minds, that they can cross the barriers which have been self-inflicted. And through the crossing of that self-inflicted barrier, all things become possible. In fact, that is what a leader is meant to do: a leader is meant to create deep confidence within people. But that can only happen when he has a deep confidence within himself.

In many ways the greatest leadership attribute is clarity—when the leader is not clouded by the non-essential. This is very important to remember. Wisdom lies in recognizing this fact of essential vs. non-essential effort and energy. The problem with us is that we are so burdened by the non-essential, that we are constantly dissipating energy. And the most efficient way to leak one's energy is through getting involved with non-essential thoughts: to become fragmented in our view, to keep being obsessed with what has happened in the past, what may happen in the future. If we can drop this and concentrate on the present moment—which is the only essential thing we have, and the only truth available to us—then all the doors of life open to us. We become strengthened at our very roots, and we can cross all obstacles with far more ease and a lot less burden in the heart.

People are always going past obstacles with a feeling of dread, or a feeling of fear within their hearts. But that is not the way of the warrior. The way of the warrior is to give up inner turmoil. When you give up your inner turmoil, the path becomes clear for you. That is what Krishna constantly tells Arjun to get rid of—his inner turmoil. Then the very quality of mind—and the very quality of heart—changes. You feel a warmth of courage within yourself. So really it is all about not being filled with theories, thoughts, or fears, but instead getting rid of them beyond a point. And that is something you simply have to will yourself to do. It's your choice, if you truly want to move towards your greater success.

The mystic code is simply to understand that you are to let your essential vitality and the power of your soul shine out. But that is only possible if you are not manipulating your own self at the level of thought and mind. The real thing lies beyond your imagined thoughts. The real power of yourself lies in the vastness of your soul. And to manifest that power of yourself, what is truly needed is to burn the non-essential thoughts within you like a fire. You know, the symbol of fire or Agni is very important in the old Hindu philosophy. It is really a metaphor for the fire we can create within ourselves, to get rid of all the non-essential and all that is not needed. So be like fire: burn the non-essential. And then what you're left with is your essential self, your essential power. And you are able to work with a more continuous and effortless flow in life. When you achieve this natural flow, you automatically move to a state where you are much closer to the heart of your cosmic and universal destiny.

The greatest religious quality in life is to get rid of the

non-essential and realize that eventually this existence of ours is a great opportunity and a great mystery. Through this feeling of wonder is born a very pure and vital energy in you. All the ancient paths of spirituality in the past have always emphasized that we are to become once again as children, who can look at things with wonder and not think we know everything. And neither should we think that the answers lie in our thoughts. The answers always lie in the subtle spiritual domain, but we can 'know' this subtle spiritual domain in a small way if we open up our minds enough by simply getting rid of the non-essential. Then only does space and broadness happen within us. And this space becomes filled with a far greater spontaneity of energy, which allows us to move towards greater success. Live the truth of the 'essential' you and not the falsehood of the imagined and thought-created worldview which society has conditioned you with. When you destroy that which is not needed at the level of thought, then does the resurrection of your true power happen.

CHAPTER-13

Welcome All Things

LESSON: Never be afraid to welcome change into your life! Change is the order of nature: it is up to you to cultivate the right attitude to it, and not be overwhelmed by it. In our era of epidemics, economic uncertainty, and ecological destruction, this lesson is key. Swami Ji lived through so many changing aspects during his own life: scientifically, geopolitically, locally, and globally. He weathered all and showed us how to evolve through change. Accept circumstances and use them as a device to awaken your utmost inner energies and creativity. That is the mark of truly successful people and great leaders.

Vivekananda used to say that the true person of spirituality is one who can welcome all circumstances within his or her life. In other words, the essential mystical and spiritual understanding is that we accept whatever comes our way. Only through acceptance does transformation happen. So the idea is that the real courage of both the sage and the warrior is not of feeling scared of circumstances, but of being prepared and able to face whatever he or she encounters. The universe has given us sufficient might to deal with things, and sometimes it is only in our crisis situations that our best qualities surface. So this is an essential key not only for spirituality but also for leadership and success in life.

In fact, true realization of leadership and success potential happens only when you have this sort of attitude within yourself. Otherwise, your spirituality is only skin-deep, it does not mean much. Essentially it is all about courage but it is also about understanding with the depth of your being that you have infinite and pure power to deal with things, if only you do not keep complaining about them. So the way is not of getting discouraged or distracted, or going into a mode of complaining with what comes your way in life. But instead using your capacity to go beyond all hindrances. Be in a thankful mode to the cosmos, because it will keep sending you new opportunities and rare moments within which you can utilize yourself more fully, and deal with things as they are.

The spiritual understanding of things is that within all things exists the essence of what we call God or the ultimate. That which in Vedanta is called Brahman. In Vivekananda's view, he is very clear about this primacy of

Upanishadic teaching which teaches that within yourself is such a totality of perfection that it cannot be shaken by circumstances. And this is the message he has left for the Ramakrishna Mission, his creation, his institution which is for social upliftment as well as spiritual upliftment of people. The monks of the mission are essentially on a path where they naturally and spontaneously have a full acceptance of life, and through this acceptance they are able to embrace whatever circumstances they are faced with. So it is a warrior sort of attitude, where the thought of the enemy is not meant to disturb one at the inward level. The warrior looks at the enemy as an opportunity for his own qualities to come out, and to transcend his self-limitations. Live the moment as it is: in any case, the next moment is absolutely uncertain. So really living in the moment means being able to stand firmly on your own feet, without getting dislodged by anxiety or nervousness. And when you can stand on your own feet with confidence there is simply no power which can disturb your inner splendour.

So it is the quality of your inner splendour which you must remember when you are faced with things. This sustains you at an emotional, psychological, and spiritual level. The very awareness that you are to be open to reality as it is, brings a very qualitative difference to how you face up to it. You have to do it with an openness towards challenges and risk, an openness to vulnerability. Then only do you become strong. Then only does people's belief in you get strengthened. The real spiritual purpose of life is to live the moment as well as you can, no matter what.

It's about remembering that each moment is an opportunity to find the play of the infinite through all sorts of circumstances. The infinite may come in the form of favourable circumstances or unfavourable circumstances, but a person of mysticism knows that each moment can be a revelation of higher truth. And when you look upon moments as revelation of higher truth, the greatest truth within yourself is revealed in the way you think and act in the world. When the great power of truth starts becoming revealed through your thoughts and actions, there is nothing to stop you from flowering to your complete potentiality. And that is essentially what success means.

So have the purity of heart and mind to not be anxious about facing things. Because only in that is there true courage. It is as the samurai of Japan say, that sometimes it is not good to be very sane! Sometimes it is good to be insane! And to have an insane kind of courage, which allows you to simply rush in where others fear to tread! That is the real, essentially dynamic attitude towards life: to go in with a sense of urgency and such swiftness of thought, that even fear does not have time to hinder or restrict you. This quality is in fact the hallmark of all great leaders and truly successful individuals.

CHAPTER-14

Rely on Your Individuality, Not on Your Ego

LESSON: Swami Vivekananda exemplifies the beauty and spiritual power of non-egoism. Ego is simply your reaction to societal conditioning: it is not your true nature. You are in reality a bliss-filled soul. Shake out of ego in order to realize your highest life and leadership potential. This is a very fundamental principle of Indian spirituality, as well as of the deepest mystical paths worldwide.

At the very root and core of Vivekananda's teaching is to have the courage to walk alone. Be completely an individual, he used to say. Even if you are part of an organization or a movement you must bring your own intelligence to it, instead of being led by a sense of ego of belonging to a particular order or set of people. Essentially each human being has an individual divinity within them. This is a very fundamental tenet which Vivekananda awakened and sought to instil within people. He used to say that only those who are immature act out of ego. A truly mature person acts out of a space where their own growth is not hindered. The only way of unhindered growth is to act out of a completeness and totality of your own individual qualities. And that essentially is the entire spiritual wisdom of Vedanta. It is about removing the barriers which prohibit your individual growth, and the biggest barrier is nothing but the barrier of ego.

In Vedanta it is said that the real psychological illness is the illness of ego. It creates the maximum damage to your own individuality and to your intrinsic fearlessness because it means that you are not functioning out of your true consciousness, your true divine intelligence, and fullness of being. But rather you are functioning out of the dream of the ego, with all its attendant fears and imaginings. You are not essentially free in your action when surrounded by egoic feeling, and that is the way you become more and more closed. It does not allow you to feel nourished by that invisible cosmic energy which is constantly vibrating in every atom of existence. Incredible joy, courage, and ecstasy are to be found from working out of an egoless space. Renounce the ego and move into a rejoicing of your individuality. Then only does your true potential take wing and move towards a natural fulfilment of itself. The ego is born of the mind but essentially all spiritual impulse is born out of purity of heart. Now, what this means is very metaphorical: it is not about the brain and the heart as physical organs, but really it's about working with an integrity of spirit. Working in a manner that you are not full of unessential fears and anxieties which keep feeding the ego. It means that you begin respecting the essential consciousness that you are made of, and stop identifying with the material circumstances you have been placed in.

Most people are so obsessed with the circumstances that they have been placed in, in life, that they become full of complexes. Either a feeling of superiority towards others, or a feeling of inferiority crops up. But all complexes are born of the ego's hidden fears. The spiritual person is one who is free of complexes. And being free of complexes is the way to make extraordinary things happen, because then everything you touch starts becoming almost a miracle. Everything you attempt starts moving faster and deeper, and you become a much better problem-solver because your essential energy is involved in your action. And because you are free of egoic fears, you go over the need to identify with your failures and defeats.

A person like Vivekananda is never 'defeated'—no matter what the circumstances—because he keeps on working with a smile within his heart. He works as if he's only a messenger for a greater power, and then does all action become delightful, blissful. Other people become more profoundly affected by him.

So to be a real influencer you must have this ability to let go of your ego, and let your inner light flow effortlessly and fearlessly, with great energy. Human beings have a hidden intuition to be able to understand the energy of others. And when that energy is pure, then happens a true relationship between people. In modern society too many of our leaders do not act out of their true individuality, or out of their deeper qualities. They unconsciously or consciously act out of a mask of character which they wear: a persona or a personality which they want us to believe they are. And that really does not translate into much good. Rather, it creates confusion in society, because it does not come out of self-realization. Such leadership remains not deeply rooted but rather shallow in its approach.

The whole art of truly positive leadership essentially depends upon removing the boundaries between people. And that always begins by removing that boundary wall of ego which exists between your outward action and your inner being. Be more connected to your authentic self. Then do you have the ability to connect to people—to relate to people—in a deeper way, to be balanced in your action. And out of this balance comes about not only balance in the work you attempt, but also a deep sense of balance and contentment in your inner being. So essentially, to be able to lead others you must be able to lead yourself to a place where you can be true to your own being, where you can find a unity within yourself, where you can make effort through the essential and authentic power within you. And that is the space which is free of ego. That is the space of pure joy, of timelessness, of your innate spiritual qualities. Function from that which is within you at the deepest core, because in that invisible energy is available all the strength of the cosmos, all the natural universal energy that exists at the core of creation.

CHAPTER-15

Realize Your Own Worthiness (Atma-Mulya)

LESSON: You are a child of a wondrous universe, born to express something unique! Never doubt that. Always keep this secret deep within your being, and be conscious of it. It will catalyse your self-power in all your life and leadership roles. Throw out the habit of constant self-doubt about your own worth and value.

One of Vivekananda's most crucial teachings was to make people realize their own self-worth *(atma-mulya)*. He used to say that life is all about knowing that you are really worthy, that you can participate in this universe with great confidence, provided you have a sense of self-dignity. Be strong, he used to say. Know that you are a child of the cosmos, and let nothing stop you from your true destiny.

This teaching is a very fundamental part of Vedanta philosophy. It is really about not allowing others to determine your sense of self-worth, about not allowing society to decide how you should act and what you should be. But rather about making yourself as you are *meant* to be as you yourself feel. This is what Vivekananda called man making. It has got nothing to do with man or woman but it's got everything to do with realizing your own self-growth and the beauty of your own being. You are your own authority. Yes, you can absorb learnings from different people. You can absorb education from many quarters, but essentially the heart of Vedantic insight is to see your own sense of inner strength. And that is also the cornerstone of true leadership and true success: to be able to understand that deep within you is all capability. Deep within you resides a profound power, which can make all your questions disappear.

So really, leadership ability is dependent on this inner revelation of being. That is what a truly positive and evolved leader is meant to be, to manifest their inner being to the maximum. It is like creating your own sculpture from all that has been given to you. You are the sculptor of your destiny. God or the Ultimate has given you enough strength to sculpt your destiny as you want. So let that be your ground-level realization. And then do you come into contact with the real force within yourself. That force is what takes you to the goal.

It's about the simple principle of being clear about your own self; of not being in a confusion about whether you are weak or strong, because essentially everybody is carrying a great fountain of immense strength within themselves. But there are very few who realize this within themselves. And those who do realize this, become truly successful in life, in every way: in the material sphere and in the spiritual sphere.

The problem with us is that we keep comparing ourselves to others. Out of this comparison, we forget that incomparable power and force resides within us as individuals. Even great people doubt themselves. Doubt is good, but life is too short to keep on doubting! Sometimes we just have to make a breakthrough. That breakthrough happens when we realize our inner force, and let this force express itself like a great light around us. So before a dialogue with others, it is a dialogue with our inner being which is important.

Strength is throbbing in your soul. Allow its vibrations to reach into the greater part of your existence. This is not an intellectual concept or a sentimental thought: this is really grounded in the ancient understanding of what human beings are. They are a fragment of divine force, and being a fragment of divine force they carry a part of that immense creativity and strength which exists in the divine and the vast. That is your original face, and that original face is capable of meeting all circumstances with great courage.

In the Bhagavad Gita, Krishna constantly reminds Arjun to be in his own natural state. To find his *swadharma*, which is his essential nature. And out of that essential nature comes a tremendous power, to move ahead with dynamism in the world. That way, we begin to undertake our tasks in an intrinsically strong manner. It is a great ecstasy—in fact the greatest ecstasy—to find this inner strength in you. But most of the time it is covered by layers of anxiety, fear, ego, jealousy, and so on. Go beyond them, transcend them, and see that at the heart of yourself you carry the strength of the boundless cosmic ocean. And make this perception the very background of yourself. Everything else is in the foreground: like a film projected onto the screen. But at the very background is that pure empty screen, and on that screen you can create the movie of your life.

Man is in this sense his own creator. Because he carries the power of the Creator within him. And there is no better creation than the act of creating oneself as one is meant to be! It is not about feeling an egoistic sense of self-importance. But rather more about realizing the unlimited sources of energy within yourself. For only then can those energies dance—only then can those energies indulge themselves with abandon in whatever they encounter.

The sense of victory or defeat is always a self-created one, because essentially the only true victory worth having is the victory of realizing your innate strength. And when you realize your innate strength, the miracle is that you absorb and receive more and more strength from the universe. It is a reciprocal process. But it all begins with understanding your own power, your spiritual power. And this understanding gives you the greatest possible bliss, because it removes the false illusion of separateness from the power of the entire cosmos. You are joined to the universe in a great bond, and its power manifests through you. So never look at yourself as less than being cosmic and universal in your scope and sense of strength. That is the bedrock of success and of successful leadership.

CHAPTER-16

Be Undisturbed!

LESSON: Vivekananda symbolizes undisturbed and infinite soul-power in the face of all life's troubles and anxieties. It is the secret of real leadership strength.

There were many occasions in Vivekananda's life where he was extremely provoked by opponents. In several instances, these opponents even made remarks about his race. Quite often he was badgered for expounding ancient Indian thoughts in the West, too. There were so many attacks on him from various quarters, yet in spite of sometimes wanting to retaliate, Vivekananda always managed to somehow remain deeply undisturbed. He used to tell his brother monks that it is not right to disturb your inner being just because of an outward disturbance. Let the outward disturbance be external: don't let it become internal. And that in fact is the very secret of balance in temperament and focus in action.

It is almost like enacting a part: each person is like an actor playing a part. But in the middle of your lines, you do not have to let them affect you internally. The dialogue remains a dialogue. It happens like a script. But the whole thing is that you are almost acting. And that is the basis of Indian mystical philosophy. The spirituality of Hinduism says that we are all actors in this divine play. And so too does somebody like Shakespeare say the same thing: 'All the world's a stage, And all the men and women merely players.' So it is meaningless to become inwardly frustrated, and disturbed in the space of your inner being. That is what self-control is: to be able to not get caught up by reactions.

Most people, when they are insulted by others, react really fast. But the person of consciousness is one who summons the greater divine energy within himself or herself, and chooses not to be disturbed. In fact, even in the life of spiritual giant Jain Tirthankara Mahavira, there were several instances where he was tortured and put to physical pain. But people were amazed at how he was not disturbed by them! He just walked on. So too was the Buddha. He used to say that it is up to us whether to accept an insult or not.

So, remaining undisturbed is really a very fundamental teaching at a spiritual and at a material level. Make it your life's code. Do not forget this, and then you will notice that within the centre of your being things become integrated. You feel a sense of strength, and this is the strength of inner integration. It allows you to behave externally in a manner which is actually beneficial not only for you, but for others also. Eventually, in a leader it is the sense of remaining inwardly undisturbed which is the most charismatic ability. The best leaders are they who can be so undisturbed, that people start having more and more confidence through their presence. So essentially it is a spiritual quality to imbibe. But the results of it are extremely beneficial at every level.

In Vedanta, being inwardly disturbed is described as a state of unconsciousness or a state of sleep. It is like dreams or nightmares disturbing you. But a person who is aware and alert can see through the dream, and realize that he is much more than them. This sense of realization is the heart of the art of a warrior: be it in Krishna's Bhagavad Gita giving advice to Arjun, or in the Japanese Buddhist samurai code of Bushido. Be it in the Greek concept of Stoicism propounded by theorists who accompanied Alexander to India (and learnt from the ascetics there), or any other 'warrior code' in the world. It all begins with remaining extremely focused and undisturbed. And that also is the secret of Arjun's being able to find the mark during the *swayamvara* (competitive marriage ceremony) for Draupadi: an undisturbed focus on the task at hand.

In twentieth century warfare you will find people like General Rommel being highly honoured for this sort of inward attitude. It is the only way to get past anxiety. It is the only way to truly deal with crisis. Otherwise the disturbance will be so great that you will be constantly involved with circumstances, instead of being peaceful and at ease within yourselves. Feeling a certain peace and ease within yourself frees up your energy to be dynamic. It creates an aliveness and an abundance in your inner life, which leads to more and more infinite possibilities in your worldly life also.

So, non-disturbance is born out of a sense of inner alertness. It is born out of a sense of being patient, being ready for the changing patterns of the world. Everything in the world changes constantly. But what is unchanging is that eternal dimension within you which is part of the cosmic consciousness. Allow that part to be so conscious, that no frustration can set in within yourself.

People become insecure and afraid by outer circumstances. But the true yogi as described by Krishna and the Bhagavad Gita is simply one who can transcend the state of fear and insecurity by becoming inwardly calm. And throughout his life, Vivekananda cultivated this to such a degree that people used to feel almost astonished by his level of ability in dealing with extreme attacks upon his character or his value system. You see, Vivekananda had gathered the strength to not only travel throughout India under the most extreme circumstances, but also to go out to West, which was in many ways not welcoming of Easterners (especially those who talked about religion). There have been instances when he lost his papers, when he had to sleep in a railroad freight yard, when he had to face hunger and cold. But even in the midst of all that, he was completely undisturbed. There is a famous story about how he once encountered the Maharajah of Kapurthala who looked down upon him in Chicago, but Vivekananda's attitude was to shrug this all off! To not let it disturb him. The only thing he used to get disturbed by was people's suffering. He used to identify very deeply with people's suffering. But that was born out of a sense of compassion. And compassion is in itself a very strengthening virtue. So if at all you have to become sensitive, be sensitive to the needs and wants of others because that is the hallmark of a great leader. In all other matters, be so undisturbed within yourself that you go on to more and more healthy states of mind and spirit. Because that is what essentially helps you become a greater success and a better leader in life.

CHAPTER-17

Give from Your Heart

LESSON: Life's greatest qualities—courageous sharing, empathy, love, beauty, peace—stem from the heart. Never sacrifice or forget this in your leadership roles. It is what makes life worthwhile.

One of the greatest virtues in human life according to Vivekananda, is to be able to give freely from your heart. Create such heartfelt, good energy within you that this energy becomes copiously plentiful and overabundant. And when your energy is abundant, then all around you you're able to create abundance.

Vivekananda always emphasized selfless service. But this is not the kind of selfless service which so-called moralists use to promote hidden agendas, to promote a religion and so on. It is simply a question of creating a goodness in energy within yourself. The principle is that within man resides a basic energy: call it the Shakti, call it the Kundalini, call it the Adi Purusha, call it the essential consciousness. And this energy is supposed to move higher and higher in the psycho-spiritual system of man. Then only does it ultimately bring the individual her or his own freedom and potential-realization. So real 'richness' in life is an evolution in the psycho-spiritual sphere. And when there is evolution in the psycho-spiritual sphere, you are able to truly become a gifter of good things to the world. And that is what a positive leader is. That is what leads to true and enduring success. Now, goodness has nothing to do with moral attitude as such. Rather, it is about making the roots of yourself so strong, that you are automatically able to make your efforts bear fruit. The resultant force of the root system brings forth the flowers of the tree.

Hence, it's not all about richness in the outer sphere, but of making yourself so rich in the inner sphere that everything you do and express spontaneously becomes more abundant and more fulfilling—not just for yourself but for your society, for your entire ecosystem. So this conversion of vision—from the outer to the inner—this turning in, is what is needed. The ability to see deeply within yourself is needed, because within you resides an unlimited share of universal good. You just have to allow it to function through you. You just have to allow the energies to climb higher within yourself. And then do you move not only towards realization of abundance through all your material actions, but even more importantly perhaps towards the spiritual aspect of life. So make the heart the very centre of yourself, because that is the thing which empowers your greatest impulses.

It is not so much the desire to succeed in life which goes into the making of truly great men. Vivekananda demonstrated this. It is the openness of heart also. We can see this in action in the lives of somebody like Abraham Lincoln or Nelson Mandela. They succeeded because they gave and served deeply from the heart, with the courage of the heart. That not only transformed their own selves but also the nations they led.

The greatest growth happens when we share. Vivekananda used to keep exhorting his monks and sannyasins to become aware of the divine phenomenon within themselves. This divine phenomenon is simply manifested through the art of giving of our best energies amidst any action, not through manipulating. Manipulators and cunning people always believe that they are smarter than others. But eventually they become poor in spirit, un-joyful, because they do not give freely from their hearts. The true bliss and joy of life happens when you are able to change—towards something higher than your routine circumstances. And that is what leadership is all about. If you project the light of bliss and wisdom from within yourself, people feel attraction towards that light of being. They begin to feel energized by your presence.

Ultimately, the art of charismatic leadership is the ability to share your inner light. And it is the light of heartfulness which is your greatest inner light. In the pages of history, Vivekananda has been known as one of the most powerful teachers, but also as somebody who fundamentally and profoundly transformed the lives of millions of people. His Ramakrishna Mission continues with that aim: to make people give of themselves as much as they can in the best way possible within the ecosystem and the society they exist in. Otherwise, even our inner potential becomes a burden, because it comes to no good for the world. It only grows if you take it away from mechanical acts of material acquisition and put it into the creative act of giving with much grace. As a result, material abundance too is bound to follow!

Always remember that you have been given much by the universe. In his encounter with John D. Rockefeller, Vivekananda very clearly told him that all the wealth Rockefeller has, has been given to him by the cosmic power—to be held in trust so that he can share it with others. So that he can give from within his heart, in a positive manner, to the world.

And that is what happened: Rockefeller began a process of philanthropy which uplifted millions in various ways. He became a very good living example of how material life can be balanced with great spiritual vision. It's not about doing philanthropy: it's about giving whatever energy one has, to the fullest. It has a reciprocal effect.

It requires tremendous courage to give from the heart, but it is simply a question of adjustment in attitude. In the spiritual vision of Vivekananda, material progress and spiritual progress can go hand in hand! That has to be the credo for positive leaders in today's world, and in the future, if we want a better future for humanity and earth.

CHAPTER-18

Don't Identify with Negative Emotions

LESSON: *Man's preoccupation with negative emotions and thoughts is his greatest weakness. Get rid of this preoccupation, and you emerge fresh, strengthened, empowered! Discard the negatives constantly from your mind: it's the most effective means to leadership clarity and excellence.*

Vivekananda was often asked about how to deal with usual human problems, especially those related to anger, jealousy, and various other urges or emotions. How should we function freely, with focus (the *ekagra* state) and without emotional turmoil? Vivekananda used to give very Vedantic answers, explaining that while these things are natural to the human condition, the essential spiritual thing is that we should not *identify* with them. Because eventually, the true essence of our being is that of a witness, of a pure consciousness which is not to be identified with these fluctuating emotions or feelings. That way we transcend the problems and function freely, dynamically, creatively, and productively.

About his own celibacy or abstinence from sex, Vivekananda taught that it is not about being anti-sex, but more about knowing that you don't have to identify deeply with these urges. Because through identifying, what happens is that your energy often gets confused. People keep wasting their time in getting identified with things like jealousy, for example, comparing themselves to others. And in the whole process they pull themselves down. Now you have to remember that in Vivekananda's own life he abstained from sex, yet he never judged other people on this point. He was continually interacting with householder disciples. He had a very natural (and in fact an often playful, witty) interaction with so many people. He was rather relaxed and childlike in his ability to relate to people. But the essential thing is that he did not allow a lot of negative emotions to come in his way, because negative emotions are what prevent greatness.

Accept your emotions as they are, but remember that you are to transform your consciousness into something higher and greater than the usual emotional problems of man. And the moment you can transmute your energy into a greater purity, you find that you are able to do so much more! Now, all this seems easy to say, but what it essentially implies is that the gross energy of things like anger and sex are to be transformed into creative energy at work. Empty yourself of the need to identify with whatever mood you are undergoing. Then, you come closer to mystical realization and start understanding yourself better.

A root problem of much of the violence which takes place in the world is that people keep pouring their energies into negative emotions. And they identify themselves with these negative emotions. While it is only natural that we all have moments of fear, of weakness, what is not all right is to have a very neurotic obsession with these things. If we obsess, these negative emotions become very limiting.

Always remember that the secret is to try all possible ways to create a joyful energy within you! Because joyful energy has the most power. In the Bhagavad Gita, Krishna exhorts Arjun to go joyfully to battle. Not out of a state of tenseness. Not out of a state of anger towards his enemies. But almost like he is enacting the part which the Divine has willed for him. So in that way and in that spirit, even the warrior can move towards a battle without being destructive or negative in his emotions. Hence it is not the *act* of battle or sex or anger which is essentially the limiting factor. The limiting factor or the hindering factor is when you believe the various desires to be yourselves. You are much more than these. And when you realize you're more than these, you acquire great confidence within your being.

So the whole heart of confidence—which is at the base of truly successful living and leadership—is to understand that you are an ever-free being. You are much more than what you think yourself to be! Your real business should be to not condemn yourself because of negative emotions or even your natural desires, but to transform these very energies into creative acts. The problem with much of society is that it has divided things into good and bad. But most of our lives are lived in grey areas. There is good and there is bad. There is no ideology or action which can be called perfect. Life is a constant conflict. But if in the very heart of your being you attain clarity and non-conflict, then do you utilize your potential in a much higher way. And that is why spirituality is so important in your life.

Most people spend too much time fighting with their own emotions and their own selves. That way, they become weakened and inwardly divided, within the core of themselves. And when within the core of yourself you feel divided and weakened, the energy to fight it out in the world starts dissipating. You become feeble, and you are not able to move towards the highest success you are capable of. Neither are you able to inspire confidence as a leader. On the other hand, by simply remaining unidentified and without pretensions, you become free. And through this freedom comes about dynamic action and success.

CHAPTER-19

Love Is Your Natural State

LESSON: Mankind's real hunger and thirst in life is for love. Emit a radiance of loving empathy with others: it is the greatest secret of leadership charisma.

Of the numerous teachings of Vivekananda, some of his most profound are on Bhakti Yoga or the yogic teaching of love and devotion. Now, basically in the ancient Hindu understanding, love or *prema* is supposed to be a natural state yet the most under-utilized state. Most people do not bring enough energy of love into what they do, or into their relationships, which is why most people feel drained of energy. They don't feel the exuberance and enthusiasm to be as dynamic as they are meant to be. Love implies being receptive and sensitive to all that is. And that is what true human evolution is. At the end of the day, despite all his intellectual prowess and his emphasis on Vedanta philosophy, Vivekananda was known as a person who was very soft at heart. In fact, he has been known to cry, to weep for others out of compassion and love. So he was a human dynamo whose very foundation was the state of love or prema. And that is how he is transcendent to many teachers of Vedanta. He was never hard-hearted. He used to say that in his exterior he is a man of Vedanta, but in his interior he's a man of bhakti or divine love. Perhaps that explains the immense energy that he had, and the immense ability to lead people on to a new vision of life. What we must learn out of this is that essentially we are to allow love to permeate more and more into our work and into our being. That way, all our work becomes worship. All our relationships become filled with gratitude and meaning, and we are able to produce things of value within the world. Eventually, all meaningful relationships must have a feeling of mutual respect, of affection and friendliness, but that is only possible if there is some degree of love within one's heart. Because that transcends all momentary problems.

The greatest leader is one who has great love for his people. This principle applies to all things. If we are truly to be human beings of value and move towards our greater success, we must make alive the vitality of love which flows in our spiritual being. Doing so, our image of ourselves also improves. Not only that, but we are able to invest much more feeling and passion into our work. And doing so, our work gets more and more creative. So at the heart of creative pursuit is love. This does not only mean artistically creative works such as music and so on. It means any kind of work—scientific, commercial, any field in which we want maximum positive results to flow.

What love does is bring peace as a spontaneous emotion into people. At the root of the world's problems is a dearth of love, which is why the factor of 'service' has remained much underutilized in society. People simply don't either love themselves or the world as much as they possibly can. So one must look at experiencing the vastness of affection in one's heart. This affection can be towards any pursuit that one does, because then it becomes full of life. Then it becomes full of passion.

To have a passion for excellence requires us first of all to have a passion for life and what we want to achieve. Passion is at the root of fulfilment in any pursuit or career. No matter whether one is a doctor, a teacher, a mathematician, a scientist, a businessman, or an engineer, the feeling of deep love for work is really what bridges us to the divine impulse.

Visualize yourself as somebody who is capable of investing more and more love into all that you do. Project this feeling of love, and you find that people become spontaneously attracted to you. It is the vibe we transmit to others which translates into our charismatic ability. Some people enter a room and we are immediately attracted to their presence. It's because they project some sort of affection, some sort of compassion and good feeling.

At the base of all this is the human ability to bring infinite feeling of well-being into our acts. And there is no great healer of problems than the loving impulse. The very vibration of love creates a supportive situation for others. One starts being looked at as more reliable. It not only heals one within oneself, but also brings others closer to us in thought and spirit. From a mystical and spiritual point of view, to find our true centre of being or the true core of our soul, is not possible without going deeply into the feeling of love. Because then only comes about the possibility of relating to life in a deeper manner. All the mystics of the world have said so. The impulse of love is both timeless and infinite in man. It allows the mind to roam free. It allows us to not feel isolated from life, but to come closer to it. And with this feeling of coming closer to nature and to the world, we become more confident people. Because we feel that everything is imbued with much value. And we are able to enter into a deeper dialogue not only with other people, but with life itself. It creates a feeling of relaxedness within us. It is about being able to flow in a creative manner, and that essentially is the root of all fulfilment.

CHAPTER-20

Live as If It is Your Last Moment

> *LESSON: The core spiritual teaching that Vivekananda stressed was to live as if every moment were your last. He considered this the very root of all excellence. Imbibe this dynamic lesson deep within, making it part of your personal life and leadership credo.*

Vivekananda used to advise people to live with a clear awareness that death can come at any time. Hence, we are to make complete use of the moment, of whatever time we have left! Living in this urgent, intense yet spiritually established manner allows one's hidden potential to surface to the maximum.

In more recent times, Steve Jobs of Apple Inc. beautifully echoed this core spiritual teaching during his speech to students at Stanford University: he considered it the very root of all excellence! The consciousness that our time on earth is limited, truly puts things in perspective and focus.

Man's greatest illusion is that he has a long time to go before he dies. But the person of spiritual understanding knows that life is very transitory. It moves very fast. In order to be whole in your energy, there must be a sense of urgency. Urgency gives rise to dynamic action.

Vivekananda lived a very short life. In fact, he had predicted for himself that he would die before the age of forty. And that's exactly what happened! He was not even forty years of age when he passed away. Yet he lived his life as if his work was extremely *urgent*. And that is the only way to harmonize your energy into a great laser-like force, and harness its power in such a way that you are totally focused on what you need to achieve.

It is all about bringing utmost passion and energy to the moment that you are living, because then comes real insight. Then comes a harnessing of your innermost depths of consciousness and energy. The problem with religions—throughout man's history—is that they have lulled him into a sense of the 'hereafter' (heaven, rebirth, and so on). This has made humanity restrict its consciousness, because the only true way to live is to absorb and to express as much consciousness within the moment as one can. There is no better way of inner growth—and outer growth—than to realize that what has to be done, must be done in the moment! That is the way of awakening your best qualities.

It is a waking up and a bringing into focus all the clearness and clarity of yourself to that which you are doing *now*. And it's very interesting that if you can transcend the worry of death at every moment in your life, only then do you live truly blissfully, joyously. Only then do you live to the maximum. You don't put things off for the future. Rather, you allow your energies to move with wholeness and totality. And in the process, bring your authentic nature to radiate through your actions.

It is extremely important to look directly into the situations which confront you and to bring such alertness to them, so that your subconscious worries and fears automatically melt away. That is what dynamism means. Otherwise, we keep repeating the same patterns of life. What we did yesterday, we do today. It's only when we realize that life is like a tightrope walk, within which we have to be continually balanced every moment, that we attain the greater truth of our self-potential.

It is the intensity of living which matters eventually. Not the length of time spent on earth. Therefore, make your energy so luminous that you have the guts to encounter all sorts of circumstances and situations. You would have noticed that people who have a truly radiant personality seem to have a sense of fearlessness in the face of the most dangerous situations. That is the one quality which all of us human beings can admire. And that is what the code of the warrior is all about.

As the samurai in Japan say, the whole of life is a movement towards a glorious death. It is *how you live* that matters, and not *how long* you live. That is the most ultimate and profound mystical teaching, because then only do you have gratitude for what you have in the moment. Otherwise, you're constantly in a complaining mode. You're either moving backward or forward—backward into the past or forward into the future. You do not work with a wholeness of yourself, because your mind is divided between past and future.

Essentially, to really appreciate life means that you begin shaping your destiny with an openness of heart and mind to the very fact of death. That is the greatest teacher. That is the warrior's way. And only then does death become truly irrelevant. This is the secret of strength. And through this, you can transform yourself to a situation where you are able to live and function to the maximum.

'Maximum living' demands a maximization of focus on the present moment. Every leader worth his or her salt knows this. The opportunity to live life in a great manner exists in the present moment, and not in the future. That is simply a way of postponing the essential. Don't be dictated by the normal state of your consciousness, which believes in the illusion of the future. Rather, begin understanding that what you have now is all that is. You may or may not be able to experience this again. In the old religions, the concept of resurrection—of being born again—is a very powerful metaphor. It has been used in Vedanta, it has been used in Christianity, in Buddhism, and so on. It is really all about getting rid of the fear of death. And that implies bringing enough courage into the present moment, so much so that you feel nothing can stop you!

Be like the mystic warrior Vivekananda was: fearless and grounded in the moment. Through this attitude you will come to a greater dimension of life. Then, you will be able to function with a greater freshness of response to whatever you are faced with. People who can confront life with a freshness of response, are able to bring much more meaning and value into what they are doing. They spontaneously move toward greater productivity, excellence, and success.

CHAPTER- 21

Intuition Means Clearly Opening Up to Cosmic Energy

LESSON: Swami Vivekananda was an intuitive giant, who could effortlessly connect intellectuality and spirituality. Which is why his message remains timeless and enduring. The greatest leaders and most successful people don't just rely on intellect: they supplement it with the power of intuition that is within!

Intuition is one of the greatest differentiators between truly successful leaders and others. It is intuition which brings clarity and understanding to things. Great leaders are those who can use the capacity of intuition to a maximum degree. Vivekananda used to describe intuition as not only a spiritual quality that takes man to a super-conscious level, but also as a means of functioning in the immediate circumstances one is confronted with. There have been numerous examples in his life where he used intuition to a tremendous degree. When he began reading a book given to him by a scholar, and when the scholar questioned him about the book a short while later, he was surprised to find that Vivekananda knew every passage he was questioned on. Such was his super-conscious intuitive ability. We all have such intuitive ability in some measure: the question is how we realize and put to use even a small portion of it!

What is the secret of intuition? Intuitive capacity according to the mystic vision arises by opening the mind ('freeing' it) completely to existence. This openness helps us read more deeply into things. This in fact is the whole basis of spiritual understanding. All human beings who have attained a higher consciousness have been able to demolish the barrier of the limited brain, and move into that which we might call the intuitive field where abides ultimate reality.

What this implies is that 'intelligence' as we know it, is not about simply gathering knowledge. It is actually about listening deeply to cosmic intelligence, and thereby functioning according to it. While this may seem vague or arbitrary, what it implies is that you recognize that there is a factor within you which is comprised of immortal, timeless consciousness. And once the understanding of this cosmic factor within you takes root, you are able to see beyond the normal consciousness of human beings.

The real challenge is to understand that energy can move in infinite ways. Our human knowledge and understanding is only a small part—a small reflection—of the real truth which is facing us. Now, how does this correlate to success in material life? It has a very deep resonance for being an achiever, because it implies that we need an upsurge of our consciousness in order to tap into our infinite potential. It implies that we are to function not according to outer 'knowledge', but according to the self-knowing which arises within our being. The whole understanding has to be that we are to function in accordance with our fundamental self. And when we function as our truer fundamental self, content within our being, then does our true universal intuition work.

Intuition implies being more and more aware of the deeper truths of life. But in order to activate your intuitive power, it is important that you do not become too occupied with your usual anxieties and fears. For it is when you are not occupied by anxieties and fears that your intuition begins to act in a deeper way. Then does your intelligence become the temple of intuition. Then only can you contemplate higher things.

Now, leaders as such are not necessarily intuitive.

But truly *positive leaders* are those who can be so clear in mind—with the indefinable quality of intuition at work—that their thoughts and actions are not contradictory to each other. And if their thoughts and actions are not in contradiction, they can even manifest the power of a seer, a rishi! The idea is: become a person whose inner functioning reflects his/her outer functioning. That is the whole secret of being integrated and centred in thought and action, where you are not worried about the irrelevant, but come to an understanding that your greater purpose is to serve the world in the capacity of your own individual self.

We are all here with a hidden purpose. But because of our pretensions we tend to complicate things, and miss the truly courageous way of seeing what our own lives are meant to achieve. Forget the established ways of doing things. Forget the conditionings that you have been raised up with. Forget the fears that you have been encountering throughout your years of education and living in society. And then only do you attain a courage which awakens your intuitive capacity.

At the end of the day, an individual like Vivekananda is a revolutionary against that which is the accepted or the status quo. He challenged the notions of 'knowledge' in an age which saw massive developments in human civilization. He was a true 'disrupter', because he said that the intuitive realization of the ancient rishis (seers) was in consonance with modern science. So we can see that when a person uses subtle perception or intuition, he or she can be a true disruptor or 'thought leader'. That is what all leaders should aim to be: thought leadership is the leadership of the present and the future. But it's possible only by bringing both intuition and 'knowledge' together.

Ultimately, intuitive capacity implies transforming the very way you perceive the world. It happens by a deep acceptance of the mysterious, wonder-filled, or mystical side of life and of your being. This broadens you, frees your mind, awakens your dormant capacities. In the present day, our intelligence is constantly damaged by distractions of society, politics, and so on. If only we can see that we are to unload ourselves of the great mental burdens that society places upon us, then do we realize that we have the capacity to act more intuitively. Otherwise we keep living a rather artificial life.

Become involved in a state of being that allows you to not be caught up in the limited mental construct of your own conditioning. Then only does your intuition awaken, and you become alert to the greater consciousness of life. So doing, not only do you deep down fulfil yourself, but you also start becoming more of a contributor and positive influence upon your ecosystem and society that you live in. It is not about being passive, but rather about being so active within your inner being that you can constantly perceive yourself as being capable of winning every battle. The capacity of intuition is infinite and timeless. It can unlock our innermost capacities and solve our constant inner conflicts, thereby leading to an 'inner victory' of being. And where there is inner victory, there is bound to be outer victory. Both 'inner' and 'outer' victory define truly evolved, dynamic leaders. And these are the kind of people that Vivekananda believed in.

Acknowledgements

I wish to express my humble gratitude to the people who have made this series possible:

Anuj Bahri, my super literary agent at Red Ink.

Shikha Sabharwal and Gaurav Sabharwal, my wonderful publishers at Fingerprint! Publishing and their team.

Garima Shukla, my amazing and brilliant editor.

Family—my parents, partner Sohini, sister Priti, nieces, nephews, et al: you are my rock.

Gratitude also to my support team, friends, mentors, and well-wishers over the years.

Pranay is a mystic philosopher. He is an expert on Indian and world spirituality.

Pranay's modules on 'Advanced Spirituality for Leadership and Success' (PowerTalks/MysticTalks for public and corporate audiences) have won global acclaim.

Pranay is also a theatre personality and playwright. His original productions such as *From Kabir to Kavi* and *Soul Stir* have been acclaimed by world luminaries for their path-breaking spiritual content.

Pranay and his partner Sohini run the socio-cultural philanthropic commune TAS, whose initiatives such as 'Theatre Against Drugs' (for addicts), 'Geetimalya' (for underprivileged children) and 'Shohaag' (for women empowerment) are well-known and have become movements.

Presently, Pranay is collating his discourses on mind-body-spirit themes for various book series.

Connect with him on his website: pranay.org